Personal Licence Holder's Guide

Second Edition

Scotland: For both on- and off-licence premises

Scottish Certificate for Personal Licence Holders at
SCQF Level 6 (7104-11)
Scottish Certificate for Personal Licence Holders at
SCQF Level 6 (Refresher) (7104-21)

About City & Guilds

City & Guilds is the UK's leading provider of vocational qualifications, offering over 500 awards across a wide range of industries, and progressing from entry level to the highest levels of professional achievement. With over 8500 centres in 100 countries, City & Guilds is recognised by employers worldwide for providing qualifications that offer proof of the skills they need to get the job done.

About Alcohol Focus Scotland

Alcohol Focus Scotland is Scotland's national alcohol charity working to reduce the harm caused by alcohol. Alcohol Focus Scotland provides training for people working at all levels within the licensed trade in Scotland. All courses meet the necessary legislative requirements.
0141 572 6700
enquiries@alcohol-focus-scotland.org.uk
www.alcohol-focus-scotland.org.uk

Equal opportunities

City & Guilds fully supports the principle of equal opportunities and we are committed to satisfying this principle in all our activities and published material. A copy of our equal opportunities policy statement is available on the City & Guilds website.

First edition published 2007
Second edition published 2014
Reprinted 2014 (three times), 2015

ISBN 978-0-85193-300-9

Publisher: Fiona McGlade
Development Editor: Frankie Jones
Production Editor: Lauren Heaney
Cover and book design by Purpose Ltd
Typeset by Saxon Graphics Ltd
Printed in the UK by Cambrian Printers Ltd

British Library Cataloguing in Publication Data

A catalogue record is available from the British Library.

Publications

For information about or to order City & Guilds support materials, contact 0844 534 0000 or centresupport@cityandguilds.com. You can find more information about the materials we have available at www.cityandguilds.com/publications.

Every effort has been made to ensure that the information contained in this publication is true and correct at the time of going to press. However, City & Guilds' products and services are subject to continuous development and improvement and the right is reserved to change products and services from time to time. City & Guilds cannot accept liability for loss or damage arising from the use of information in this publication.

City & Guilds
1 Giltspur Street
London EC1A 9DD

0844 543 0033
www.cityandguilds.com
publishingfeedback@cityandguilds.com

Contents

Introduction to using this book

This book is written as a guide for those who are seeking to gain their Scottish Certificate for Personal Licence Holders at SCQF Level 6 (7104-11) and the Scottish Certificate for Personal Licence Holders (Refresher) at SCQF Level 6 (7104-21) qualifications under the Licensing (Scotland) Act 2005. It covers both on-licence and off-licence premises.

It contains all the required content for the Personal Licence Holder and Refresher qualifications, plus additional material that may be useful to you in the management of your premises.

You can use this book in a number of different ways:

- You are expected to read it before attending a training session. Please note the Refresher course will not cover all of the topics that you may be tested on.
- It is a good idea to have the book with you in the training session. You can refer to it as needed, and it's a good place to make any notes so they're at hand for future reference.
- It is also recommended that you re-read the book after taking your qualification with a view to seeing if you need to make any changes at your premises.

We hope that you will find this book interesting and useful.

The exams for the Personal Licence Holder (PLH) and Refresher qualifications are slightly different. The following table explains these differences.

Topic	Number of questions in the PLH exam	Number of questions in the Refresher exam	Page reference
Introduction	0	0	*
The importance of the Act and the relationship between licensing and health			9
Overview of the licensing function	1	1	
The five licensing objectives			9
The meaning of alcohol			57
Broad understanding of what licensing legislation covers			10

Licensing law

Licensing law

Know your rights and responsibilities

One of the licence holder's biggest responsibilities is to ensure that alcohol is being sold responsibly and within the law. That means knowing who you can legally sell alcohol to, under what circumstances you can sell it, and who you must refuse to sell to.

Legally, as a licence holder, you are at liberty to refuse to serve anyone. This part of the book sums up the key things you need to know about your responsibilities – and your rights – under the Licensing (Scotland) Act 2005.

Licensing (Scotland) Act 2005

The purpose of liquor licensing is to regulate the sale of alcohol in order to minimise harm.

Scotland has a relatively new Licensing Act – it only came into force in September 2009. When the old law was being reviewed, the Nicholson Committee set up to do this was given the following terms of reference:

- to review all aspects of liquor licensing law and practice in Scotland, with particular reference to the implications for health and public order
- to recommend changes in the public interest, and to report accordingly.

The Nicholson Committee's recommendations led to the Licensing (Scotland) Act 2005. We can see that from its very beginning our legislative system is focused on health and public order. The Act sets out five high-level 'licensing objectives'. All have equal weighting and decisions about licensing must be made with reference to these five objectives:

1 preventing crime and disorder
2 securing public safety
3 preventing public nuisance
4 protecting and improving public health
5 protecting children from harm.

Did you know?

At the time of writing the Air Weapons and Licensing (Scotland) Bill is going through parliament so there may be further changes to legislation.

Further amendments to licensing legislation were made by the Criminal Justice and Licensing (Scotland) Act 2010 and the Alcohol etc. (Scotland) Act 2010. These changes have been included in this guide.

In the Act 'alcohol' means spirits, wines, beer, cider or any other fermented, distilled or spirituous liquor over 0.5% ABV. It doesn't cover alcohol 0.5% or less, the aromatic flavouring essence Angostura bitters or alcohol contained in liqueur confectionery. (For more details, and a full list of what isn't covered, see Part 3 'Alcohol'.)

The Act makes provision for regulating the sale of alcohol, regulating licensed premises and other premises where alcohol is sold, and for connected purposes. It covers all liquor licensing matters including the licensing objectives, licensing bodies and officers; licensing of premises and people to sell alcohol; licensed hours, control of order and offences on licensed premises; conditions that apply to premises and control of irresponsible alcohol promotions; and training requirements. It is a 'dual licensing system', meaning both the premises and the person must be licensed.

Licensing officials

The Licensing Board

There is one Licensing Board for each council area, or division of a council area. The local council elects members to the Board from among its council members, or councillors. The Board must have between 5 and 10 members – each council decides the number it needs. Members will elect a chair, known as the convener. A Clerk, who must be a solicitor or advocate, is appointed by the council and is responsible for providing legal advice to the Board. Board members must gain a training qualification (one day's training plus an exam).

Licensing Boards have powers under the Licensing Act to determine whether or not to grant licence applications. This includes premises licences and variations, personal licences and renewals, and occasional licences.

The Licensing Board hears any review of an existing premises or personal licence and decides what action should be taken. In carrying out their functions, Licensing Boards must seek to uphold the five licensing objectives.

The Licensing Board must hold meetings in public, which need to be publicised well in advance. The Board is allowed to delegate certain decisions to one or more of the following:

- a sub-committee
- a single Board member
- the Clerk
- a member of the Clerk's staff.

These decisions include the granting of occasional licences and personal licences or renewals where there are no offences or objections, and minor variations of a premises licence.

Each Licensing Board must write a statement of its policy, to be published every three years, and the Board can add supplementary statements. They must consult with the Local Licensing Forum, the Health Board and others. The policy:
- must seek to promote the licensing objectives
- can give a general approach to the making of licensing decisions
- should give guidance on the hours that are likely to be granted to types of premises
- must include a statement as to whether there is overprovision of licensed premises, or a particular type of licensed premises, in any locality.

Each Licensing Board must also keep a publicly available register, the 'licensing register', which shows full information about all licences and any decisions the Board has made regarding them.

The Local Licensing Forum

Each local council must establish a Local Licensing Forum for its area or division. The functions of the Local Licensing Forum are to:
- review the operation of the Licensing (Scotland) Act 2005 and how the Licensing Board operates in that area
- review the exercise of the local Licensing Board's functions
- give advice and make recommendations to the Board.

However, the Forum cannot make recommendations on any particular case. The Licensing Board must have regard to the advice of the Forum and they must give reasons if they choose not to follow it. The Board must also provide statistical information to the Forum if requested.

Forums must meet at least four times per year. Licensing Boards must hold a joint meeting with the Forum at least once per calendar year.

The local council must appoint between 5 and 21 members to the Forum. At least one Licensing Standards Officer (LSO) for the council and one person

Did you know?

When determining if there is overprovision, the Board must consult the licensed trade, residents, the Health Board and police.

from the relevant Health Board must be a member of the Forum. The other members should include people who represent the interests of:

- licence holders
- the chief constable
- people having health, education or social work functions
- residents of the area
- young people.

The Forum must elect a convener annually.

Licensing Standards Officers

Each council must appoint one or more Licensing Standards Officers (LSO) for their area, who will report to the Licensing Board, liaise with other council departments and be a member of the Local Licensing Forum. The LSO must undertake a prescribed training qualification (around three days' training plus an exam). The LSO has three main functions:

1 Guidance	Providing information and guidance to interested persons (eg licensed trade, public) concerning the operation of the Licensing Act in their area, although they cannot give legal advice.
2 Compliance	Monitoring compliance with the Act by licence holders.
3 Mediation	Providing mediation services to avoid or resolve disputes or disagreements between licence holders and any other persons.

You must allow an LSO to enter your premises at any time, although they're likely to keep visits to normal opening hours. They can inspect any substances, articles or documents relating to licensing legislation found there. Licence holders, premises managers or anyone working on the premises must provide the LSO with assistance and information, and produce documents as requested. Failure to do so (without reasonable excuse) is an offence.

If an LSO believes a condition of a licence has been breached, or has received a complaint from a member of the public, they can investigate the matter. They can apply to the Licensing Board for a review of the licence. Normally they will first ask for improvements to be made. If not enough is done the LSO will then issue a compliance notice requiring the situation be rectified. You

must deal with any such notice in the specified timescale. If the matter is not resolved satisfactorily, the LSO will then make an application to the Licensing Board for a review of the premises licence (see page 21).

Premises licence

A premises licence is issued by the local Licensing Board in whose area the premises are situated, and authorises the sale of alcohol on the premises. It governs what activities are allowed and what hours the premises can be open for business.

The applicant

To apply for a premises licence, you must be at least 18 years old.

There is a check to see whether applicants for premises licences (and also personal licences, see page 22) have any convictions for a relevant offence or foreign offence (spent convictions are not counted). In addition, police have the ability to comment to the Licensing Board on an applicant's suitability with regard to the five licensing objectives.

If you are convicted of a relevant or foreign offence while the application is being processed, you have a legal duty to inform the Licensing Board within one month. Once you are a premises licence holder, if you are charged with an offence, you have a duty to inform the court that you are a licence holder, and if convicted then again you have a legal duty to inform the Licensing Board within one month (the court must also inform the Board). It is an offence if you fail to inform either the Licensing Board or the court.

The list of relevant or foreign offences is a long one. It includes violent offences, sexual offences and statutory offences – such as offences under the Trade Descriptions Act, Food Safety Act, Betting, Gaming and Lotteries Act, Drugs Act, Firearms Act and Traffic Act – as well as common law offences such as breach of the peace, contempt of court and perjury. For more information, ask your local Licensing Board.

Application process

Your application to the Licensing Board must contain:
- a description of the premises
- a layout plan

Did you know?

A premises licence is for the premises where alcohol will be sold. There is no limit on the number of premises licences a company or partnership may hold.

- an operating plan
- certificates for planning, building standards and food hygiene if food is supplied.

Layout plan

Your layout plan must include:

- where alcohol will be sold
- where activities will take place
- any area to which children and young people will have access.

Operating plan

Your operating plan is a detailed plan of how you intend to run your business. In the plan you must include:

- a description of all activities to be carried out
- whether alcohol is to be sold on or off the premises (or both)
- the proposed capacity of the premises
- name and address of the premises manager, who must be a personal licence holder and should be the person taking day-to-day responsibility for the premises (a person cannot be a premises manager for more than one premises at a time)
- (on-licence) whether children will be permitted and, if so, what ages will be permitted, and details of when and where they will be allowed to enter
- core times when alcohol will be sold and any seasonal variations.

The operating and layout plans will form part of the premises licence. If you forget to put anything in your operating plan, you will not be allowed to do it unless you apply for a variation of your licence. On receipt of the application, the Licensing Board will notify people with a notifiable interest in neighbouring land, community councils, the local council, police, Health Board and fire authorities for the area. The Board will have a hearing to consider the application, taking into account any objections or representations received from interested parties. Any person can object to an application, no matter where they live. They can also make a representation. A representation can either support the application or ask for modifications or conditions to be added. Objectors can argue against the licence on any of the five grounds for refusal listed below. The Licensing Board can reject any objection if it is considered 'frivolous or vexatious'.

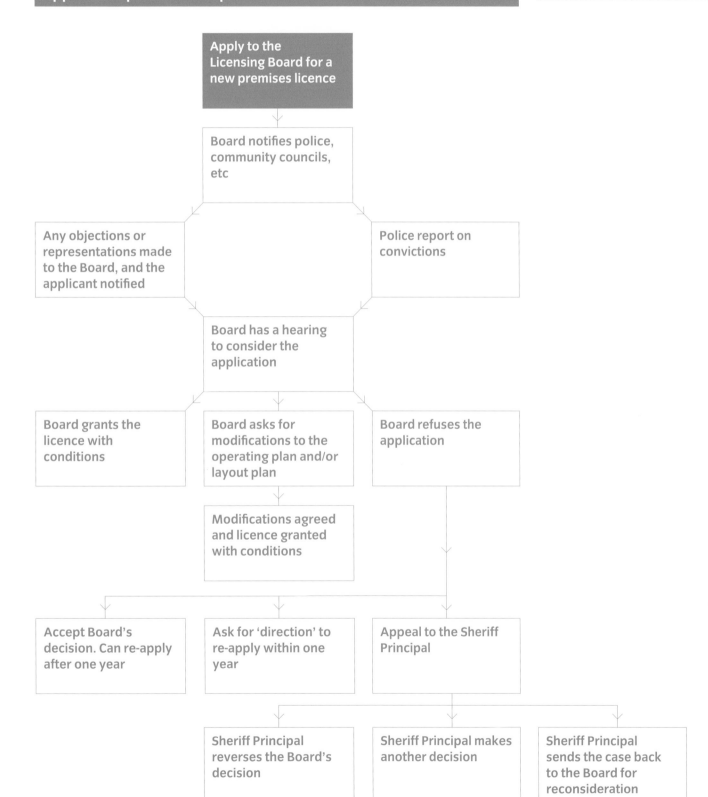

Apply to the Licensing Board for a new premises licence

Board notifies police, community councils, etc

Any objections or representations made to the Board, and the applicant notified

Police report on convictions

Board has a hearing to consider the application

Board grants the licence with conditions

Board asks for modifications to the operating plan and/or layout plan

Board refuses the application

Modifications agreed and licence granted with conditions

Accept Board's decision. Can re-apply after one year

Ask for 'direction' to re-apply within one year

Appeal to the Sheriff Principal

Sheriff Principal reverses the Board's decision

Sheriff Principal makes another decision

Sheriff Principal sends the case back to the Board for reconsideration

Grounds for refusal

Licensing Boards can refuse an application on the following grounds:
- the premises in question are an excluded premises (eg a motorway service station)
- the premises are unsuitable for the sale of alcohol
- granting the licence is inconsistent with any of the five licensing objectives
- granting the application would result in overprovision in the locality of the licensed premises
- the same application was refused within the last year and no direction granted.

The Licensing Board will list how they will seek to promote the five objectives and the sort of hours they would normally grant in their licensing policy. If your application is against the Board's policy, this could be grounds for refusal. If no grounds for refusal apply, then the Licensing Board must grant the application.

The Licensing Board issues the premises licence and a summary of the licence. Once granted, the premises licence lasts indefinitely, unless revoked, suspended or varied. It's your job to make sure it isn't.

If the application is refused, another application cannot be made within one year for the same premises unless:
- at the time the application was refused a direction was granted by the Licensing Board to allow a resubmission within a year, or
- it can be shown there has been a material change in circumstance.

Beyond this an appeal against a Licensing Board's decision can be made to the Sheriff Principal at the Sheriff's Court, but it is advisable to get legal advice before proceeding as the appeal must be on very specific grounds.

Conditions

Every premises and occasional licence has conditions attached. There are three 'levels' of conditions: mandatory national conditions that apply to all premises, national discretionary conditions (also known as pool conditions) and local conditions. The Act gives Scottish Ministers the power to add to the list of national conditions as they feel necessary. Such changes would normally be covered in the licensed trade press and the LSO would also provide advice. The national conditions, plus any local or discretionary conditions applied, become part of the premises licence. Breach of any of the conditions may lead to a review of the licence.

Mandatory conditions for all premises

Mandatory national conditions for both on- and off-licence premises include:

- Alcohol cannot be sold on the premises when there is no named premises manager, or when the premises manager does not hold a personal licence, or when his/her personal licence is suspended, or when his/her licensing qualification does not meet the requirements of the law. [Members' clubs are exempt; not applicable to occasional licences.]
- The premises must be run in accordance with the operating plan. [Occasional licences must be run in accordance with the terms of the licence.]

- Every sale of alcohol must be authorised by the premises manager or another personal licence holder. (They can give a general authorisation for all staff to be able to sell alcohol – they don't have to supervise each sale.) [This applies to an occasional licence if it was issued to a premises or personal licence holder; members' clubs are exempt.]
- All staff (paid or unpaid) who sell or serve alcohol must have been trained, and whenever they are working a record of their training must be available on the premises to produce to a Licensing Standards Officer. [Not applicable to occasional licences.]
- The price of alcohol can only change at the start of the licensed period, and the price must stay the same for at least 72 hours. Note: off-sales premises can start individual price changes on different days. [Also applies to occasional licences.]

- Voluntary organisations can only be granted an occasional licence for an event in connection with their activities.
- All premises must operate an age verification policy based on age 25. [Also applies to occasional licences.]
- No irresponsible drinks promotions are allowed (see page 19). [Also applies to occasional licences.]
- Premises licence fees must be paid annually to the council. [Not applicable to occasional licences.]
- Multiple purchases must cost at least the same as buying the items individually. [Also applies to occasional licences.]

Mandatory conditions (on-licence)

Mandatory national conditions that apply to on-licence premises only include:

- Non-alcoholic drinks must be available for purchase at a reasonable price. [Also applies to occasional licences.]
- There must be a notice (at least A4 size) displayed so that it is reasonably visible to customers entering the premises, stating whether or not under-18s are permitted on the premises, and if so, where on the premises they are permitted and any conditions relating to them while there. [Not applicable to occasional licences.]

- Tap water fit for drinking must be provided free of charge on request. [Also applies to occasional licences.]
- For premises that permit admission of children under five, there must be baby-changing facilities that are accessible to people of either gender. [Members' clubs, vehicles, vessels and moveable structures are exempt.]

Mandatory conditions (off-licence)
Mandatory national conditions applying only to off-licence premises include:
- Alcohol can be displayed in only one or both of the following – a single area as agreed between the Licensing Board and the premises licence holder, and/or a single area that is not accessible by the public, eg behind the counter. [Not applicable to occasional licences.]
- Drinks promotions can only take place in the designated area for alcohol sales or a designated tasting room. [Not applicable to occasional licences.]
- Drinks promotions cannot take place within 200m of the boundary of the premises. [Not applicable to occasional licences.]

Mandatory conditions for late opening premises
These conditions apply to premises open after 01.00. Between 01.00 and 05.00 (or close, whichever is earlier) they must have a first aider on the premises. In addition, between 01.00 and 05.00/close, premises that have a capacity of 250 or more and provide music, dancing or entertainment must have:
- a personal licence holder on the premises
- written policies on drugs and evacuation of the premises
- CCTV
- monitoring of toilets
- an SIA-qualified door steward at every entrance.

Discretionary conditions
Discretionary conditions are nationally set conditions from which Licensing Boards can choose the one(s) they think relevant to their area or particular premises in their area. At the time of writing, these have not been set.

Local conditions
Local conditions give Licensing Boards the flexibility to deal with local issues or circumstances. Where they are imposed, they must be consistent with mandatory national conditions. Examples of these may be: no entry onto the premises after 23.00; no off-sales to people under 21 on Friday and Saturday after 16.00; no drinks on the dance floor.

Licensing Boards also have the power to vary the conditions for some or all of the premises in their area.

Did you know?

Licensing Boards are not allowed to impose a blanket ban on off-sales to under-21s in their area, although they can add it as a condition to an individual premises, eg when reviewing their licence.

Irresponsible drinks promotions

This list, which also applies to occasional licences, may be added to over time by the Scottish Government:

- any promotion likely to appeal to a person under 18
- anything that involves a free or reduced price alcoholic drink with the purchase of one (or more) drinks, which don't have to be alcoholic
- anything that involves a free or reduced price measure of an alcoholic drink with the purchase of one (or more) measures of the drink (on-licence only)
- providing unlimited amounts of alcohol for a set price (including the entrance fee) (on-licence only)
- anything that encourages a person to buy or consume larger measures than they had intended (on-licence only)
- anything based on the strength of alcohol
- anything that rewards or encourages people to drink alcohol quickly
- anything that offers alcohol as a prize/reward (unless that alcohol is in a sealed container and then consumed off the premises).

What do you do with your premises licence?

When granted, the Licensing Board will send the premises licence and a summary of the licence to the applicant and a copy of the premises licence to the chief constable.

The premises licence holder is responsible for ensuring a summary of the licence, or a certified copy, is publicly displayed. The premises licence holder has a duty to keep the full premises licence, or a certified copy, on the premises. It must be shown to the police or LSO if required. The premises licence is an important document with key information including:

- the name and address of the premises manager
- the name and address of the premises licence holder
- a description of the premises for which the licence is issued
- the date on which the licence takes effect
- the operating plan and the layout plan for the premises, including licensed opening hours
- the conditions to which the licence is subject (or a reference to where the conditions can be found).

Don't forget the premises licence holder has a duty to notify the Licensing Board of any change of name or address of the licence holder or premises manager within one month. Failure to do so is an offence.

Premises manager

Every premises must have a named premises manager. A person can only be the premises manager for one premises at a time, and the premises manager must be a personal licence holder. They are responsible for the day-to-day running of the premises.

Transferring a licence to a new owner

When selling licensed premises, the premises licence holder must make an application to the Licensing Board to transfer the premises licence to the new owner, or transferee. However, if the licence holder becomes insolvent, incapable or dies, or if the partnership is dissolved, then the transferee makes the application. A copy is then sent to the police, who have 21 days to report to the Licensing Board on the transferee.

If the transferee or connected people have no relevant convictions, and there is no recommendation for refusal, the Licensing Board must grant the application. Otherwise, a hearing will be arranged to consider the application.

Variations of a premises licence

A premises licence holder can apply to vary the premises licence, eg if you wish to change your hours, or add or remove something from the operating or layout plans. If you are considering any alterations to the premises, make sure that you have all the required permissions. These include building warrants and planning consent.

Applications for a variation of the premises licence are made to the Licensing Board and must be accompanied by the premises licence. Minor variations have to be granted by the Board. Normally this is done under delegated powers. These include:
- variation of the layout plan, as long as the change is still consistent with the operating plan
- restricting the amount of access for under-18s
- any changes relating to the premises manager.

All other variations are colloquially known as 'major variations'. These include applying to change a condition or to change how the premises operates (eg from a restaurant to an off-sales). Major variations are similar to a new licence application, and are subject to the same grounds for refusal and the same rules for appeal and re-applying. The Licensing Board must hold a hearing to make a decision. You can apply to transfer and vary the premises licence at the same time.

Did you know?

You must inform the Licensing Board of any incoming or outgoing person(s) who are connected to the business within one month. You must also notify the Licensing Board of changes in names or addresses – the Board must inform the police.

Varying the premises manager

If the premises manager ceases to work for a company, becomes incapable or dies, or has their personal licence revoked or suspended, the premises licence holder must notify the Licensing Board within seven days. They must also make an application within six weeks to vary the licence to substitute a new manager. The applicant should mark on the application that it is to have immediate effect. This will allow the application to be deemed granted and allow the new manager to take up their position straight away. Remember: if there is no active premises manager, no alcohol can be sold.

Review and possible suspension

Anybody may apply to the Licensing Board to have a premises licence reviewed, although they must state why they are applying for the review. It's a good idea to remember this when dealing with disputes with neighbours. The grounds for review are:

- one or more of the conditions have been breached
- the operation of the premises is compromising one or more of the licensing objectives.

The police, LSO and Licensing Board can also initiate this procedure.

Upon receipt of an application, the Licensing Board will consider whether the application contains grounds for review and arrange a hearing if necessary. The Board can reject any application to review a premises licence if it is thought to be frivolous or vexatious. If the Board finds, during the review, that you are not complying with certain conditions of your licence or are running the premises in a way that is inconsistent with the licensing objectives, they can take the following steps:

- issue a warning
- make a variation to the licence (such as reducing your opening hours)
- suspend the licence
- revoke the licence.

Personal licence

A personal licence allows you to supervise or authorise the sale of alcohol. Every premises must have one premises manager and the premises manager must be a personal licence holder. Most premises, however, are likely to employ several personal licence holders to ensure there is always a qualified person present.

Training required

The 2005 Act requires that a personal licence holder must have a suitable qualification. There are national standards for the training and qualification. These can be found at www.scplh.info.

If you wish to become a personal licence holder you must do a course – normally a full day – and then sit a 40-question multiple choice exam. On gaining your qualification, you must then apply for your personal licence (see below).

You must show evidence to the Licensing Board that issued your licence that you have completed Refresher training within five years of the personal licence being issued. This is a half-day course, also with a 40-question multiple choice exam. If you do not complete Refresher training, the Licensing Board must revoke your personal licence.

Ten years after gaining your licence, you must complete the full Personal Licence Holder course and exam again.

Application process

An application for a personal licence should be made to the Licensing Board for the area that the applicant normally lives in (even if the person works in premises covered by a different Board). The Licensing Board will notify the police. The application must include two photos of the applicant and the appropriate fee. The Licensing Board must grant the application as long as:

- the applicant is 18 or over and has a suitable licensing qualification
- the applicant has not had a licence revoked in the last five years
- the applicant is not already in possession of a (Scottish) Personal Licence
- the police have not issued a notice advising that the applicant has relevant convictions nor indicated that the applicant is not suitable with regards to the five licensing objectives.

The same obligations to inform the Board of any relevant or foreign offences apply as for the application for a premises licence (see page 13). If the applicant has convictions the Board can hold a hearing to determine the application. There is no mechanism for anyone other than the police to object to a personal licence application.

The Licensing Board will tell the police and the applicant of their decision. Once granted, the licence will last for 10 years, unless suspended or revoked. You must update your qualification every five years and advise the Licensing Board accordingly, otherwise the Board must revoke your licence.

Application process for a personal licence

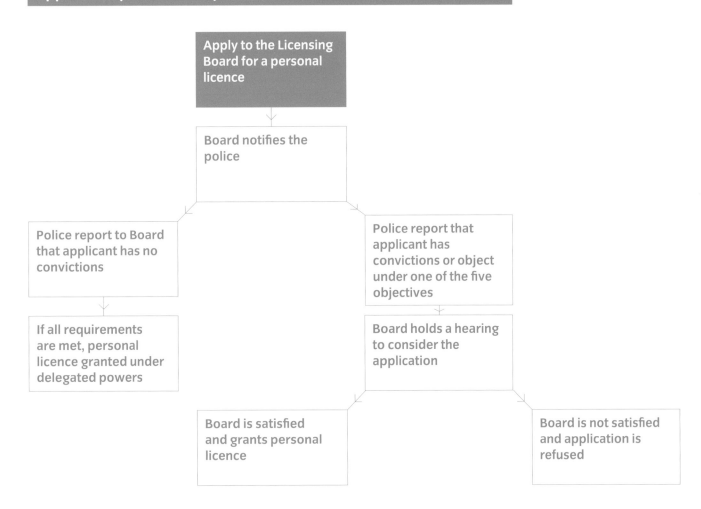

Apply to the Licensing Board for a personal licence

Board notifies the police

Police report to Board that applicant has no convictions

Police report that applicant has convictions or object under one of the five objectives

If all requirements are met, personal licence granted under delegated powers

Board holds a hearing to consider the application

Board is satisfied and grants personal licence

Board is not satisfied and application is refused

Did you know?

Premises managers need to inform the Licensing Board where they are working of convictions; other personal licence holders inform the Board that issued their licence.

What do you do with your personal licence?

The personal licence will show the name and address of the licence holder, the Licensing Board that issued it, expiry date and any relevant or foreign offence. As a personal licence holder, you have a duty to produce your licence to either the police or the LSO when working on licensed premises. You also have a duty to notify the Licensing Board of any changes to your name or address within one month. Failure to do so would be an offence. Again, exactly the same as a premises licence holder, a personal licence holder has a duty to inform the court if charged with an offence and inform the Board if convicted. The Board will then review the personal licence.

A licence is counted as void if it has been lost, stolen, revoked, or if it was granted while the person already held a personal licence issued by a Scottish Licensing Board. A void licence must be returned to the Licensing Board that issued it. It is an offence to try to pass off a void licence as a valid one.

Review of a personal licence

The Licensing Board can review a personal licence under certain circumstances, ie if the Board is informed that the personal licence holder has been convicted of a relevant or foreign offence; or if, when the Licensing Board is reviewing a premises licence, they find that the personal licence holder acted in a manner inconsistent with the five objectives. The police can report a personal licence holder to the Licensing Board for conduct inconsistent with the licensing objectives. The Board has the option to take no action, endorse, suspend or revoke the licence.

Did you know?

Unlike a premises licence, only the police can report a personal licence holder to the Licensing Board.

An endorsement on a personal licence works a bit like points on a driving licence. An endorsement lasts five years and if a personal licence holder gains three endorsements, the Licensing Board must hold a hearing to review the licence.

Renewal of a personal licence

Personal licence holders must apply for a renewal at least three months before the expiry date to the Licensing Board that originally issued the licence. The application should include the personal licence or, if not practical, a statement of the reasons why it could not be sent.

Other types of licence

Occasional licence

This allows alcohol to be sold on an unlicensed premises for particular occasions or events. Applications can be made by either a personal or premises licence holder or a representative from any voluntary organisation. Members' clubs and voluntary organisations are restricted to no more than 4 licences lasting 4 days or more, and 12 licences lasting less than 4 days, up to a maximum of 56 days in any 12-month period.

Temporary licence

The issue of a temporary licence allows a business to continue to operate in another premises while its normal premises are undergoing reconstruction or conversion.

Provisional licence

A provisional licence can be granted to premises that will be, or are being, built or converted. It is valid for four years.

Members' clubs

Members' clubs are only open to, and can only sell alcohol to, their members and guests. They are included in the same system of licensing and subject to the same rules as other licensed premises, with a couple of exceptions:

- They are required to have a premises licence, although they do not have to name a premises manager. This means that they will not require a personal licence holder to authorise the sale of alcohol. However, they still need to train staff and any person who serves or sells alcohol – whether paid or not.
- The Licensing Board will not include them in any assessment of overprovision, and they cannot be refused a licence or a variation of a licence on the grounds of overprovision.
- They don't have to provide baby changing facilities if they allow under-fives.

Members' clubs are able to apply for occasional licences (see 'Other types of licence').
On these occasions the premises can be opened to members of the public.

Did you know?

The Licensing Board may be able to limit the number of occasional licences issued to a premises of personal licence holder in the future.

Licensed hours

Licensed hours are when premises can sell alcohol, and for on-licence premises they are also the times when alcohol can be consumed.

Off-licence premises

Alcohol can be sold in off-licence premises from 10.00 to 22.00, Monday to Sunday. The Licensing Board must refuse any application that asks for off-sales outside these times. It is possible that a Licensing Board may restrict off-sales hours for particular premises if there are problems, or to fit with local circumstances. Alcohol must be off the premises by 15 minutes after the end of licensed hours.

On-licence premises

On-licences will have licensed hours determined by what is stated in the operating plan, and hours will be specific to each premises. Some Licensing Boards insist that premises are open for the hours stated in the operating plan and granted in the premises licence, but many do not. Check with your Board or LSO. The Licensing Board must refuse any request for 24-hour opening unless there are exceptional circumstances.

Extended hours (on-licence)
A premises licence holder can apply to the Licensing Board for an extension of licensed hours for their premises for a special event or occasion. The Licensing Board must notify the police and the LSO for the area when any application is made and if it is granted. In addition, Licensing Boards may grant general extensions of licensing hours for an event of local or national significance, for all or some of the on-licence premises in the area as the Board decides. The Licensing Board can vary the conditions of the premises licence for the period of the extended hours.

Exceptions to licensed hours
There are exceptions to the hours permitted in your operating plan. The main ones are listed on the next page. All of these are optional; you do not have to allow them.

Drinking-up time	A period of 15 minutes is allowed at the end of hours for consuming any remaining alcohol that has been bought during licensed hours.
Meals	If alcohol was supplied with a meal, then the drinking-up time increases to 30 minutes.
Residents	Hotel residents or their guests can drink alcohol and take it away at any time, but the alcohol can only be sold to the resident.

British Summer Time

Premises open at the time that the clocks go forward/back should ignore the change to the clock and trade for the usual amount of hours.

Staff training

Every person who sells or serves alcohol has a responsibility to uphold the law. They can be charged with offences, as can the premises licence holder (see page 32). The Licensing (Scotland) Act 2005 requires that all staff are trained before they sell or serve alcohol. This includes full-time, part-time and casual staff, and people who are unpaid. The training must cover a 16-point syllabus set by the Scottish Government. It includes the basics of licensing law, alcohol and the influence of environment in licensed premises. This training must be a minimum of two hours in length. It can be delivered in a number of ways:

- A personal licence holder or qualified trainer can deliver suitable training.
- Staff can use a workbook under the supervision of a personal licence holder or trainer. City & Guilds have produced the Workbook for Staff of Licensed Premises for this purpose.
- Staff can undertake formal training to gain a nationally recognised training certificate.

A training record for each member of staff must be available on the premises for inspection by the LSO at all times when the person is working. There is a standard format for the records of staff training, as detailed in The Licensing (Mandatory Conditions No.2) (Scotland) Regulations 2007. The training record must show the names and signatures of both the person undertaking the training and the trainer. The trainer must be either a personal licence holder or hold a relevant training qualification, accredited by the Scottish Qualifications Authority. PLHs must give their personal licence number and the Licensing

Board that issued it; qualified trainers must give the name of the qualification they hold and the company they're employed by. It is probable that a visiting LSO will ask to see these training records.

Protecting children from harm

One of your biggest responsibilities as a licence holder is to ensure that alcohol is being sold responsibly and within the law. It is a key responsibility that you do not sell alcohol, or allow it to be sold, to anyone under the age of 18.

The Licensing (Scotland) Act 2005 defines a child as being under 16 years of age, a young person as being 16 or 17, and an adult as being 18 or over.

No proof of age, no sale

The law states that all premises (including occasional licences) must have an age verification policy in place where everyone who appears to be under 25 is asked for proof of age.

If charged with selling to a child or young person, the server must be able to show that they believed the person to be 18 or over and that either:
- no reasonable person would suspect from the person's appearance that he or she was under 18, or
- they asked the person for proof of age (and what they were shown appeared to be an appropriate form of proof of age and one that would have convinced a reasonable person).

The Act says that acceptable forms of proof of age are a passport, a European photocard driving licence, a photographic identity card approved by the Proof of Age Standards Scheme (PASS), a (British) military identity card, a national identity card issued by a European country (other than the UK), Norway, Iceland, Liechtenstein or Switzerland, a biometric immigration document or any other document as may be prescribed. The most commonly available proof of age card in Scotland is the Young Scot card. Always check for the holographic PASS logo and, as with all forms of proof of age, check the date of birth. Remember you do not have to accept the proof: if you're not sure, refuse the sale.

Display notice

Under the 2005 Act, premises (including occasional licences) must display a notice regarding underage sales. It must be displayed at all times, at each place on the premises where sales of alcohol are made, and be visible to any person seeking to purchase alcohol. The notice must be A4 size or larger and must state:

> It is an offence for any person under the age of 18 to buy or attempt to buy alcohol on these premises.
>
> It is also an offence for any other person to buy or attempt to buy alcohol on these premises for a person under the age of 18.
>
> Where there is doubt as to whether a person attempting to buy alcohol on these premises is age 18 or over, alcohol will not be sold to the person except on production of evidence showing the person to be 18 or over.

Prevention system and refusals book

You must have an age verification policy, based on age 25. It is good practice to write the policy down, eg in your house policy, and to train staff on what they must do. It is also good practice to have:

- signage for staff and customers about what forms of proof of age are accepted
- proof that you and your staff refuse sales, eg by recording all refusals in a refusals book.

You should check that all of your staff know how to use the refusals book. If one person is not using it properly, then they might need training on who to refuse service to and how to do it. Keep your refusals book at the counter/ bar and make sure everyone fills it in when refusing a sale. If you get a visit from the police, you can easily produce it to show how you comply with the law. The refusals book could also contain some brief reminder points on who cannot be served alcohol, and brief tips on handling the situation when you refuse a customer.

Offences relating to under-18s

It is an offence for licence holders and staff to:

- sell alcohol to a person under 18, or for a responsible person to allow it
- sell liqueur confectionery to a person under 16
- allow a person under 18 to sell, supply or serve alcohol unless:

- □ in an off-licence premises, the sale is specifically approved by a person 18 or over
- □ in an on-licence premises, the alcohol is for consumption with a meal and the supply or service is specifically approved by a person 18 or over
- allow a person under 18 to consume alcohol on licensed premises (but see exception below)
- deliver alcohol to a person under 18, or allow a person under 18 to deliver alcohol (unless it is at their place of work and it is part of their job) or for a responsible person to allow it.

It is an offence for customers to:
- buy, or attempt to buy, alcohol if they are under the age of 18 (unless it's part of a test purchasing scheme)
- buy alcohol for a person under 18 (but see exception below)
- consume alcohol on licensed premises if they are under 18 (but see exception below)
- send a person under 18 to obtain alcohol.

Exceptions (on-licence)

Although you cannot legally sell alcohol to a young person (ie a person who is 16 or 17 years old) under any circumstances, you can allow them to consume alcohol bought by an adult if it is to accompany a meal. Only beer, cider, wine or perry is allowed and only in limited amounts. You have no obligation to serve them, but legally you are permitted to do so. It's always a good idea to have a house policy that sets out your rules on this and other matters. Make sure that your staff are aware of your house policy.

Test purchasing

Test purchasing of alcohol is authorised by the police. It allows them to send someone under 18 years old into licensed premises to try to buy alcohol to check that the premises does not sell alcohol to underagers. There is a strict code of conduct governing a test purchasing scheme. This aims to protect the welfare of the child or young person, and also aims to make the system fair for the licence holder and staff. The underage person is not allowed to try to look older than their real age, and must tell the truth if they are asked what age they are.

Other offences

We've already seen some of the offences relating to children and young people. There are other offences that you also need to be aware of. It is an offence for licence holders, staff or any 'responsible person' to:

- sell alcohol to a person who is drunk
- be drunk on the premises
- allow a breach of the peace, drunkenness or other disorderly conduct on the premises
- keep smuggled goods on licensed premises
- deliver alcohol to a private address between the hours of midnight and 06.00
- fail to display the notice regarding underage sales
- fail to display a summary of the licence.

It is an offence for customers:

- to attempt to enter any licensed premises while drunk (unless the person resides there)
- to be on licensed premises while drunk and incapable of looking after themselves
- to obtain or attempt to obtain alcohol for a drunk person or to help a drunk person obtain or consume alcohol
- for a drunk person to behave in a disorderly manner
- for a drunk person to use obscene or indecent language to the annoyance of any other person
- for a person to behave in a disorderly manner and refuse to leave or to refuse to leave at the end of licensed hours when asked to do so by a responsible person. A responsible person can use reasonable force if necessary to remove the person from the premises.

So what is drunk exactly?

There is no legal definition of drunk, so it is up to you to decide. But do remember that you may put your personal licence and possibly the premises licence at stake if you serve a drunken person. Therefore, if in doubt, don't serve them. (We will look at signs of drunkenness in Part 3 and ways of refusing service in Part 4.)

As we are all subject to the law of the land, don't assume that because something isn't listed in this book, it doesn't apply to you. A criminal conviction can affect your fitness to hold a personal or premises licence.

Did you know?

A responsible person is defined as the premises manager or occasional licence holder, or any person aged 18 or over who has the authority to sell alcohol or the authority to stop any offence from occurring.

Vicarious liability and due diligence

For most of these offences the premises licence holder is vicariously liable, meaning they can also be charged. They have a defence: they must be able to prove that they did not know the offence was being committed by the employee or agent *and* that they exercised all due diligence to prevent the offence being committed.

Due diligence is having a system in place that would normally prevent the offence occurring. A risk assessment of likely problems can be helpful to identify what action needs to be taken to prevent issues.

Further areas of law

Deliveries

If you sell alcohol for delivery to a customer you must ensure that the sale takes place within licensed hours. It is an offence to deliver alcohol to a private address between midnight and 06.00. You must keep a day book (kept at the premises) and a delivery book or invoice (kept with the delivery) that states the quantity, description and price of the alcohol and the name and address of the person it is being delivered to. Remember that it's an offence for alcohol to be delivered to a child or young person. It is also an offence for alcohol to be delivered by a child or young person, unless he or she works on the premises in a capacity which involves the delivery of alcohol.

Rights of entry

Police can enter and inspect licensed premises (including off-sales and members' clubs) at any time, and obstructing a police officer from doing so constitutes an offence. LSOs can also enter and inspect premises at any time. Obstructing or refusing to comply without reasonable excuse is an offence.

Exclusion orders

An exclusion order is an order made by the court excluding a particular person from a particular licensed premises (or group of licensed premises), and lasts between three months and two years. It applies to a person convicted of a violent offence committed on or in the vicinity of licensed premises. If an order is not imposed by the court at the time, the premises licence holder has up to six weeks after the date of conviction to apply to

have the order imposed. Anyone entering licensed premises in breach of an exclusion order commits an offence and is liable to receive a fine, a term of imprisonment or both.

Closure orders and emergency closure orders

The police can ask the Licensing Board to make a closure order requiring a premises to close. The police and the Licensing Board must be satisfied that there is a likelihood of disorder on, or in the vicinity of, the premises and that closure of the premises is necessary in the interests of public safety.

Police officers (of the rank of inspector or above) have the power to make emergency closure orders. These last a maximum of 24 hours but can be extended for a further 24 hours if required.

A police officer (of the rank of inspector or above) must terminate the order if satisfied that it's no longer in the interests of public safety. A premises or occasional licence holder can also apply to the Licensing Board to terminate the closure order – again the Board must be satisfied that closure is no longer in the interests of public safety. Notice of the termination must be given to a responsible person, and if the closure order was originally made by the Licensing Board, then the Board must also be given notice.

Vessels, vehicles and moveable structures

It is an offence to sell alcohol on a moving vehicle unless it has a premises or an occasional licence. An example would be a party limousine. Ferries or trains that are engaged on a journey are 'exempt' premises, ie they do not need a licence to sell alcohol. However, if a ferry was permanently moored, it would need to be licensed.

Safeguarding your licence

Do people get charged under the licensing laws? In a word, yes. Even where an offence does not lead to a criminal prosecution, it may still be brought to the attention of the Licensing Board, who can review the premises and personal licences.

Under a system of vicarious liability, the premises licence holder or interested party can be charged for an offence that an employee or agent commits, even if the employee or agent is not charged. Licence holders therefore need to

Did you know?

The social responsibility levy is legislation that has been passed by Parliament but is not yet in force. At some point in the future, the Scottish Government may impose a levy on premises and occasional licence holders amongst others. Monies raised will be used by the local authority to promote the licensing objectives.

show that they actively take steps to prevent offences from occurring. These could be set out in a house or store policy and covered in staff induction training.

Your house or store policy can give staff guidance on how you do things in your premises to ensure you stay within the law and prevent situations occurring. More information on common issues can be found in Part 4 of this book. Certain elements of the business, eg fire safety, have to be risk assessed. It's worth doing a similar assessment for other possible threats to your business, eg the risk of angry or drunk customers. A risk assessment could lead to a change in the way the premises operates to manage these risks. Remember: if changes mean you wish to vary your operating plan, you will have to apply to the Board to vary the premises licence. Don't forget it's not enough to train staff on arrival and give them a copy of house policy. Your staff need to understand and abide by the policies in place, and should take part in continuous training. You should also test your system – how else can you know that your staff are doing what you asked? It's your licence that will be revoked or suspended, so there's a lot riding on it. Don't be careless about it.

Self check

1 What are the **five** licensing objectives of the Licensing (Scotland) Act 2005?

2 Name the **two** main types of licence available under the law.

3 What document demonstrates how you plan to run your business?

4 Who can object to a premises licence application?

5 What are the licensed hours for the following:

   a Off-licence premises?

   b On-licence premises?

6 Who can authorise the sale of alcohol?

7 What types of proof of age are acceptable?

8 The police have the right to enter your premises at any time. Which other licensing official has the right of entry?

9 Name **three** offences that can be committed by:

   a staff or licence holders

   b customers

Test practice

1 Which **one** of the following is the body that grants premises and personal licence applications, renewals and transfers?

    a The Environmental Health Office
    b The Planning Department
    c The Licensing Board
    d The Local Licensing Forum

2 Which **one** of the following people can an occasional licence be granted to?

    a A premises licence holder, a personal licence holder or a representative of a voluntary organisation
    b Anyone who works in a bar or club selling alcohol
    c Members of registered clubs, members of proprietary clubs and representatives of registered charities
    d Anyone running an event which is on a not-for-profit basis

3 On which **one** of the following grounds can a member of the public apply for a review of a premises licence?

    a The premises is not meeting one of the licensing objectives
    b The Licensing Standards Officer has issued a compliance notice
    c The staff were rude to them when they visited
    d There is overprovision of premises of that type in the area

4 Which **one** of the following does the applicant for a personal licence have a duty to inform if they are convicted of a relevant or foreign offence while their licence application is being processed?

    a The police
    b The Licensing Board
    c The Local Council
    d A Sheriff Principal

5 A personal licence holder must undertake training

    a Only when applying for the first time for a licence
    b Yearly
    c Every five years
    d Every 10 years

6 Where and when does the law require that a notice relating to the sale of alcohol to underagers must be displayed?

   a At the front of the premises when the premises is open
   b At each place where sales of alcohol are made and at all times
   c In a non-public area where staff have their break and at all times
   d On the till receipt given to customers after a sale of alcohol

7 How would a premises know that a closure order has been terminated and the premises may open again?

   a The police must give notice to the LSO
   b The police must give notice to a person responsible for the premises
   c The LSO must give notice to a person responsible for the premises
   d The LSO must give notice to the Licensing Board

2

Other key legislation

The following section will guide you through some of the other laws that affect licensed premises. There are so many laws that not all of them have been included here. Most of the laws and regulations that are listed do require some action by premises managers or personal licence holders, but it is also important that all other members of staff are aware of their legal responsibilities.

Health and safety legislation

Health and Safety at Work Act 1974

The Health and Safety at Work Act 1974 (HASAWA) is the principle legislation in this area. In general, it applies to all businesses, no matter how small. It requires employers to ensure, as far as possible, the health, safety and welfare at work of all their employees. It also states that each member of staff is responsible for ensuring that their own working practices will maintain the health and safety of themselves and their colleagues. All staff should have access to written information outlining their responsibilities and those of their employers, which could take the form of either a poster in the staff area or an individual handout. Most businesses will also require to have employers' liability insurance.

Management of Health and Safety at Work Regulations 1999

The Management of Health and Safety at Work Regulations 1999 makes more explicit what employers are required to do in order to manage health and safety under the Health and Safety at Work Act 1974. Like the Act, these Regulations apply to every work activity.

The duties of the employer are qualified in the Regulations by the principle of 'so far as is reasonably practicable'. In other words, the degree of risk in a particular job or workplace needs to be balanced against the time, trouble, cost and physical difficulty of taking measures to avoid or reduce the risk.

An employer's main requirement is to carry out a risk assessment, which should be straightforward in licensed premises. A risk assessment identifies potential risks or hazards and how to reduce them. Employers with five or more employees need to record the significant findings of the assessment. (Employers with five or more employees must also have a written health and safety policy.)

The five steps of risk assessment are:

1 Look for the hazards (ie anything that could harm the health or endanger the safety of people on the premises).
2 Decide who might be harmed and how.
3 Evaluate the risks (what are the possible consequences, and how probable are they to occur?) and decide whether the existing precautions are adequate or whether more should be done.
4 Record your findings and implement them.
5 Review your assessment and revise it, if necessary. Reviews should take place at regular intervals as conditions may change.

As well as carrying out a risk assessment, employers need to:
- make arrangements for implementing the health and safety measures identified as necessary by the risk assessment
- appoint competent people (often themselves or company colleagues) to implement the arrangements
- set up emergency procedures
- provide clear information and training to employees
- work together with other employers sharing the workplace
- have first aid arrangement in the workplace.

The Health and Safety Executive (HSE) publishes guides to good practice and advice on how to comply with the law. See www.hse.gov.uk.

Control of Noise at Work Regulations 2005

Noise levels are measured in decibel units and are shown as dB(A). Damage risk to hearing depends on the noise level and how long people are exposed to it.

You, as an employer, are required to assess your employees' exposure to noise. There is likely to be a problem if:
- people have to shout at each other at normal speaking distance
- anyone goes home with a ringing sensation in their ears.

Where employees are regularly exposed to noise levels of 80 dB(A) or above, employers must assess the risk to workers' health and provide them with information and training. At 85 dB(A), employers must provide hearing protection. Over 85 dB(A), health surveillance (hearing checks) must be provided. See www.hse.gov.uk/noise for more information.

Manual Handling Operations Regulations 1992

Work-related musculoskeletal disorders (MSDs), including manual handling injuries, are the most common type of occupational ill health in the UK. They are preventable. The Regulations list the measures for dealing with risks from manual handling.

These are:

1 Avoid hazardous manual handling operations as far as reasonably practicable.
2 Assess any hazardous manual handling operations that cannot be avoided.
3 Reduce the risk of injury as far as reasonably practicable. Where possible, you should provide mechanical assistance – for example, a sack trolley or hoist. Where this is not reasonably practicable, look at ways of changing the task, the load and working environment.

For further information, see www.hse.gov.uk.

Food, drink and sales legislation

Food Safety Act 1990

These regulations cover every aspect of the safety of food that is intended for human consumption. Because 'food' includes drinking water, alcohol and even chewing gum, they apply to licensed premises. Since the regulations were updated in 1995, anyone who handles food or drink is required to have supervision, instruction and/or practical hygiene training to a level appropriate to their job. Premises must have a food safety management system. Hazard Analysis and Critical Control Point (HACCP) is a widely accepted system which can be adapted to suit all sizes and types of food business.

The Act contains tough powers to require improvements to be made to unhygienic premises, and premises can be closed where public health is being put at risk. It is mostly enforced by local authority officers, such as Environmental Health Officers, who have the power to enter food premises and inspect food, take samples for investigation and withdraw suspect food.

Further information and guidance can be found at www.food.gov.uk, or contact the Environmental Health Office at your local council.

Adulteration of food and drink

The Food Safety Act says that it is illegal to add anything harmful to food or drink. It is also illegal to take anything away from it by diluting it or watering it down. Watering down spirits or other alcohol is one example of an offence.

Food hygiene certificates

Under the Licensing Act (Scotland) 2005, you must provide a copy of a Food Hygiene Certificate when applying for your premises licence to the Licensing Board if food will be supplied on the premises. Food Hygiene Certificates will normally be granted by the Environmental Health Office of your local council, providing that the structural requirements of the food hygiene regulations have been, or will be, met.

Food Labelling Regulations 1996

These Regulations aim to ensure that foods are correctly labelled. Most foods require an indication of minimum durability such as a 'best before' or a 'use by' date. It is not illegal to sell food after its 'best before' date has passed, but if the product has deteriorated so that it is 'not of the nature, substance or quality demanded by the purchaser' as required under the Food Safety Act, then a prosecution could be brought under the Act. 'Use by' dates are different from 'best before' dates and it is illegal to sell food after its 'use by' date. Some foods do not need to be marked with an indication of durability. These include:

- fresh fruit and vegetables
- wine, liqueur wine, aromatised wine and any similar drink obtained from fruit other than grapes
- any drink with an ABV (alcohol by volume) of 10% or more.

Age-restricted products

Alcohol and liqueur chocolates are among a much longer list of products that can be sold only to customers above a set age.

Over 18 years old	Alcohol, fireworks (includes caps), butane gas/lighter fuel, adult magazines, offensive weapons (knives), cigarettes, tobacco, tobacco-related products.
Over 16 years old	Lottery tickets and scratch cards, liqueur chocolates, party poppers, fuel.
Depends on classification	Videos, DVDs, games.

Consumer Protection from Unfair Trading Regulations 2008

The Consumer Protection from Unfair Trading Regulations 2008 updated and replaced a range of previous legislation such as the Trade Descriptions Act and the Consumer Protection Act. Under the legislation it is an offence to apply a false or misleading description to goods. In other words, the goods you give a customer must be what is advertised. For example, you can't put another brand of gin into a Gordon's gin bottle; or if a customer asks for a particular brand, eg Coke, and you don't have Coca-Cola, you must check with the customer before you give them another brand of cola. It is also an offence to put pressure on customers to purchase products.

For more information contact the Trading Standards Officers at the local authority, or visit www.oft.gov.uk.

Protected terms
Certain products are referred to by protected terms that must be used correctly.

Champagne, Cava and Prosecco	Only wines grown in the Champagne region of France and made by the Champagne method may legally be called Champagne. You must not sell any other sparkling wine as 'Champagne'. Similarly, 'Cava' must come from Spain and 'Prosecco' from Italy.
Sherry	This is a legally protected term for fortified wines from the Jerez region in Spain. Wines from other regions or countries that used to be called sherry now have to be labelled and referred to as 'fortified wine', not sherry. (If they were bottled before 1996, they must be qualified by the country of origin, eg Cyprus Sherry.)
Scotch	It is an offence to sell as Scotch Whisky any whisky that is not made in Scotland and at least 40% ABV. Similar drinks made in any other country are normally spelt as 'whiskey'.

Non-alcoholic and low-alcohol
You must be careful when using the terms 'non-alcoholic' and 'low-alcohol', as each has a specific meaning according to the amount of alcohol present in

a drink. For example, you can't give someone a low-alcohol drink if they have asked for a non-alcoholic one, unless you check that this is acceptable with them. Please remember that, for medical or religious reasons, some people cannot tolerate any alcohol at all. All of the following have specific meanings.

Non-alcoholic	0% Alcohol By Volume
Alcohol-free	less than 0.05% Alcohol By Volume
De-alcoholised	0.05% – 0.5% Alcohol By Volume
Low-alcohol	0.5% – 1.2% Alcohol By Volume

Advertising standards

There are specific rules for the advertising and promoting of alcohol. These rules apply to you, even if you're only putting an advert in the local newspaper or producing a promotional flyer to give out in your local area. Remember, anyone can make a complaint about advertising.

There are two bodies that govern the advertising and promoting of alcohol, each dealing with different types of advertising. These are:

- Advertising Standards Authority (ASA), which deals with non-broadcasting advertising (press, posters, commercial emails, SMS) and TV, radio and cinema advertising. See www.asa.org.uk for more information.
- The Portman Group, which deals with complaints about naming, packaging and promotional material (including point of sale materials, websites, sponsorship, press releases, branded merchandise, advertorials and sampling). See www.portmangroup.org.uk for more information.

The rules for each are slightly different, but they broadly cover the same areas.

Adverts and promotions of alcohol must not:
- cause serious or widespread offence
- encourage excessive drinking
- target under-18s
- encourage daring or aggressive behaviour
- suggest that alcohol can enhance sexual success.

Weights and Measures Act 1985 (on-licence only)

Draught beer and cider	Glasses for draught beer and cider must be government stamped (unless you're using an approved measuring device). Beer and cider may only be sold in quantities of $^1/_3$ pint, $^1/_2$ pint, $^2/_3$ pint and multiples of $^1/_2$ pint. Following the Metrication Amendment in 1994, only draught beer and cider can be sold in the old imperial measures. If you wish to sell shandies or non-alcoholic drinks in a similar quantity, you can use the metric equivalents of 568ml (approximately one pint) or 284ml (approximately $^1/_2$ pint) provided that: ■ you inform the customer ■ if the drink is advertised in a price list, the metric measure is stated. Beer and cider can be sold in lined or brim glasses. The lined glass allows room for a full pint of liquid and the head of froth. The brewing industry is of the opinion that the head is part of the pint and can be up to 5% of the brim glass; however, servers should always top up the glass if the customer asks.
Spirits – whisky, gin, vodka and rum	Since 31 December 1994, the only permissible optic measure for the sale of these four spirits is metric. These are available in two sizes, 25ml and 35ml, but one size must be chosen for use. It is not legal to use both measures for these spirits on the same premises. A notice stating the size of measure that whisky, vodka, gin and rum are sold in must be clearly displayed.
Cocktails	Any of whisky, vodka, gin or rum are exempt from the above requirements if they form part of a drink which is a mixture of three or more liquids.
Fortified wines	Fortified wine, when sold by the glass, must be sold in 50ml or 70ml.

Did you know?

All optics and beer measuring devices must comply with specific regulations and be made in compliance with a current certificate of pattern approval. If in doubt, check with the Trading Standards Officer at your local council.

Did you know?

Other products, such as brandy, can be sold in other measures. However, it is common practice to offer them in the same measures as the four spirits. This makes it easy for the customer to know what they're getting and makes stock control easier.

Did you know?

In England and Wales it is a mandatory condition that customers can purchase a small measure, ie ½ pint of beer/lager/cider, 125ml glass of wine, single measure of spirits. This isn't currently law in Scotland, but is good practice.

Wines

Wines can be sold by the glass, bottle or carafe. You can display the information regarding the quantities of wine you offer for sale in every wine list or menu, or on a prominently displayed notice. Wines sold by the glass must be in specified quantities of 125ml, 175ml or multiples of either, but wine in quantities below 75ml is exempt. Carafes of wine may be sold in quantities of 250ml, 500ml, 750ml and 1 litre.

Business legislation

Smoking, Health and Social Care (Scotland) Act 2005

The Smoking, Health and Social Care (Scotland) Act 2005 is commonly known as 'the smoking ban'. It makes it an offence to smoke in wholly, or substantially, enclosed public places in Scotland. These places include workplaces, such as pubs, bars, clubs, shops, storerooms and even marquees. (There is a limited exception for designated hotel bedrooms.) It is an offence to smoke in an enclosed public place and it is an offence to allow another person to smoke in an enclosed public place. You must display no-smoking signage at every entrance to your premises, in toilets and staff areas.

You should think about how smoking impacts on your premises: litter, noise, as well as people crowding your entrance, perhaps preventing others from entering. You may want to consider providing designated exterior smoking areas with adequate facilities for the disposal of cigarette butts. You could put up notices asking your customers to be aware of the noise they make outside so as not to disturb the neighbours. You may want to consider any implications for the security of the premises if staff are going out the back to smoke.

The Environmental Health Departments of local councils enforce the legislation. For more information, see the Scottish Government's website: www.clearingtheairscotland.com.

Equalities Act 2010

The Equalities Act brings together a number of existing laws, such as those relating to disability discrimination and sex discrimination. It sets out the personal characteristics that are protected by law and the behaviour that is unlawful. People are not allowed to discriminate, harass or victimise another person because they have any of the protected characteristics. The protected characteristics are:

- age
- disability
- gender reassignment
- marriage and civil partnership
- pregnancy and maternity
- race
- religion and belief
- sex
- sexual orientation.

It is also an offence to discriminate against someone who is perceived to have a protected characteristic or who is associated with someone who has a protected characteristic. Premises must make reasonable adjustments to accommodate disabled people, and employers are responsible for the actions of their staff.

Further, both staff and managers have the right to work in an environment free from intimidation, bullying and harassment – by other staff members, managers, or even customers. Any customer who is behaving in an inappropriate manner should be asked to leave the premises. An employer can be found responsible if a customer or contractor bullies or harasses an employee.

Equal opportunities apply to recruitment, payment, treatment in the job, chances for promotion and training, dismissal or redundancy. More information can be found on www.equalities.gov.uk.

Private Security Industry Act 2001

The Private Security Industry Act 2001 outlines a system for the statutory regulation of the private security industry.

If you work in one of the roles listed below in England, Wales or Scotland, or employ someone who works in one of the roles, you may need to be licensed. This covers manned guarding, including:
- cash and valuables in transit
- close protection
- door supervision
- public space surveillance CCTV
- security guard
- key holding.

Licences are issued by the Security Industry Authority (SIA). There are two types of licence:
- A front-line licence is required if you are undertaking designated licensable activity (this also covers undertaking non-front-line activity). A front-line licence is in the form of a credit-card-sized plastic card that must be visible to the public, subject to the licence conditions.
- A non-front-line licence is required if you manage, supervise and/or employ individuals who engage in designated licensable activity, as long as you do not carry out front-line activity yourself. A non-front-line licence is issued in the form of a letter.

If your job includes door supervision activities, you need to have a door supervisor licence. It doesn't matter whether you own the licensed premises, are employed by the licensed premises or are employed by a firm which supplies door supervisors to the premises.

A door supervisor licence is required if manned guarding activities are undertaken in relation to on-licensed premises only (when the premises are open to the public, at times when alcohol is being supplied for consumption, or when regulated entertainment is being provided on the premises). A door supervisor licence is not required if the activity:
- only involves the use of CCTV equipment
- falls within the definition of cash and valuables transit.

In Scotland door supervisors are more commonly known as door stewards. For more information, please visit the SIA website: www.the-sia.org.uk. Also see the list of related qualifications in the 'Useful resources' section for City & Guilds qualifications in these areas.

Phonographic Performance Licence (PPL) and PRS for Music (formerly Performing Rights Society)

When a sound recording is played in public, there are two separate licences that must be obtained. Under the Copyright Design and Patents Act 1988, there is a copyright in the musical and lyrical composition (PRS) and a separate copyright in the actual sound recording (PPL).

PRS represents the owners (ie the writer or composer) of the music and a PRS music licence grants legal permission to play the music on public premises.

PPL authorises any 'public' use of sound recording. 'Public' is considered to be any event except a family or domestic gathering. It includes playing music for staff only, such as the kitchen of a restaurant, and even playing music to customers 'on hold' on the telephone. Playing music without a licence could result in court action.

For more information about the two types of licence, see www.prsformusic.com (PRS) and www.ppluk.com (PPL).

Gambling Act 2005

The Gambling Act 2005 regulates all forms of gambling in the UK except the National Lottery and spread betting. The Licensing Board makes decisions on licensing in its area, and the Act is regulated by the Gambling Commission.

The Act is based on three licensing objectives:
- preventing gambling from being a source of crime or disorder, being associated with crime or disorder or being used to support crime
- ensuring that gambling is conducted in a fair and open way
- protecting children and other vulnerable people from being harmed or exploited by gambling.

Under the Act, premises that are licensed to sell alcohol for consumption on the premises will be permitted to provide equal chance gaming (including poker and bingo) but are subject to strict conditions. These conditions include limits on stake money, prizes, fees and record keeping. It is advisable that you check with the Licensing Board before you allow any type of gaming or gambling on your premises. This includes traditional pub games such as cribbage and dominoes.

Amusement with Prize (AWP) machines are also strictly regulated. Different categories of machines are allowed depending on the type of premises and access by children. Procedures for application will depend on the number and type of machines. It may be as simple as informing the Licensing Board and paying a fee, or it may require an application for a permit.

Certain lotteries, draws and sweepstakes are permissible, but there are conditions attached to the prizes and the destination of the profits: they must not be for commercial gain. Some must be registered.

All gaming, whether machines or games, must be run in accordance with the Gambling Commission's statutory code of practice. For more information, see www.gamblingcommission.gov.uk.

Relevant criminal legislation

Misuse of Drugs Act 1971

This is the main piece of legislation covering drugs. It categorises drugs as class 'A', 'B' and 'C'. These drugs are termed as controlled substances, and Class A drugs are those considered to be the most harmful.

Offences under the Act include:
- unlawful possession of a controlled substance
- possession of a controlled substance with intent to supply it
- supplying or offering to supply a controlled drug (even where no charge is made for the drug)
- allowing premises you occupy or manage to be used unlawfully for the purpose of producing or supplying controlled drugs.

Drug trafficking (supply) attracts serious punishment including life imprisonment for Class A offences. To enforce this law the police have special powers to stop, detain and search people on 'reasonable suspicion' that they are in possession of a controlled drug.

Handling drug-related issues on your premises is covered in Part 4.

Self check

1 What are the **five** steps involved in carrying out a risk assessment?

2 Which regulations cover the safety of food for human consumption?

3 Name **three** products that can only be sold to a person over the age of 16.

4 Name the **two** bodies responsible for advertising.

5 What is the difference between non-alcoholic and low-alcohol drinks?

6 What measures can only be used to sell draught beer and cider?

7 Under the Equalities Act 2010, what must licence holders do to accommodate disabled people?

8 Which council department enforces the smoking ban in public places in Scotland?

9 Under the SIA regulations, there are **two** types of licence. What are they?

Test practice

1 Once a risk assessment has been completed, which **one** of the following should happen?

   a It must be reviewed at regular intervals
   b It should be stored in the safe
   c Staff should attend a health and safety course
   d It should be sent to the Health & Safety Executive

2 What are an employee's responsibilities under the Health and Safety at Work Act (HASAWA) 1974?

   a To ensure that they inform their colleagues before doing something risky
   b To ensure that there is a risk assessment for their working practices
   c To ensure that their working practices maintain the health and safety of themselves and their colleagues
   d To ensure that they have recorded their working practices in the health and safety manual

3 Which **one** of these is **not** illegal?

   a To sell food that is past its 'use by' date
   b To sell food that is past its 'best before' date
   c To sell food that is unfit for human consumption
   d To sell food that is falsely or misleadingly presented

4 Which **one** of these is included in the code of practice for advertising alcohol?

   a Advertisements should be socially responsible
   b Advertisements should encourage excessive drinking
   c Advertisements should suggest alcohol can enhance mental, physical or sexual capabilities
   d Drinking alcohol should be portrayed as a challenge

Alcohol

3

Alcohol

The recent changes to licensing legislation are one part of the Scottish Government's action to tackle Scotland's alcohol problems. In 2002 the first Plan for Action on Alcohol Problems was published and led to a review of licensing legislation and the Licensing (Scotland) Act 2005. In 2009, Changing Scotland's Relationship with Alcohol: A Framework for Action was published, leading to further legislation – mainly through the Alcohol etc. (Scotland) Act 2010. These changes are included in this guide. The Government's current alcohol policy can be viewed on www.scotland.gov.uk.

This part of the guide looks at what alcohol is and how it affects us. It explains how to calculate units, and explains low-risk guidelines for consumption. It outlines some of the common patterns of alcohol misuse in Scotland: immediate problems that can result from acute intoxication, such as injuries and violence, are covered, as well as the longer term problems linked with continued excessive drinking, such as harm to physical and mental health, relationships and employment.

What is alcohol?

Alcohol is a drug. It is a substance that affects the way the brain (and body) functions. Alcohol is a legal drug, regulated by legislation. Under the Licensing (Scotland) Act 2005, 'alcohol' means spirits, wines, beer, cider and any other fermented, distilled or spirituous liquor.

It does not include:
- alcohol 0.5% or less
- perfume
- any flavouring essence recognised by Customs and Excise as not being intended for consumption as (or with) dutiable alcoholic liquor
- the aromatic flavouring essence known as Angostura bitters
- alcohol which is, or is included in, a medicinal product
- denatured alcohol
- methyl alcohol
- naphtha
- alcohol contained in liqueur confectionery.

Alcohol is our 'drug of choice'. In Scotland alcohol is part of many key milestones and ceremonies, such as weddings and funerals, and we use it as a social lubricant. However, Scotland also has a culture of heavy drinking (too much overall) and binge drinking (too much at one time). Both lead to significant health and social harm. The majority of adults in Scotland drink alcohol, but a number of people are teetotal, ie they do not drink any alcohol.

Did you know?

The Scottish government may change the definition of alcohol to include Angostura bitters in the future.

Because alcohol is legal and widely available, many people see it as safe and tend to underestimate or be unaware of its effects. As servers of alcohol, with the legal responsibility to decide who you should and should not serve, it's particularly important that you are aware of all the effects of alcohol.

Alcohol and the body

Alcohol is categorised as a depressant drug because of the way that it works, especially on the brain.

One of the first areas of the brain to be depressed or 'numbed' is the area that controls judgement, emotions and inhibitions. This may make people more chatty or become the life and soul of the party – which is why many people wrongly believe alcohol is a stimulant. The loss of control over inhibitions and judgement is one of the effects that can make alcohol dangerous: it makes people feel unstoppable.

In fact alcohol worsens physical and mental functioning, so people are likely to be capable of less, not more, than usual. The illustration below shows the areas of the brain that become increasingly depressed as the alcohol level rises:

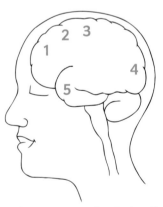

1 Emotion centre – resulting in fewer inhibitions, person becoming more relaxed
2 Speech centre – resulting in slurred speech
3 Movement centre – resulting in unsteady movement
4 Vision centre – resulting in difficulty in focusing or 'double vision'
5 Primitive brain – this is the part that keeps a person alive, the heart beating and lungs working.

If the primitive brain is affected by excessive alcohol, a person is likely to become unconscious, and this can be fatal. This is known as 'alcohol poisoning'. Information on what to do if someone collapses is included at the end of this section. You and your staff must make sure that you never serve someone this much alcohol.

All staff need to watch for the signs that someone is becoming drunk. You should discuss with your staff at what point a customer will be judged to be drunk and will be refused service. Clear guidance should be included in your house or store policy. In dealing with a drunk person, it's important to keep in

mind that they may be slower to understand than usual, and quicker to anger. Ways of handling such situations are discussed in Part 4 of this book.

When a person takes a drink of alcohol its effects begin very quickly, generally within five minutes. The liver breaks down and neutralises the alcohol, processing it out of the body. This generally begins about twenty minutes after a person starts drinking. The liver works at a consistent rate of approximately one unit per hour (although this may be slower if the person is unwell). There is nothing that can be done to speed up this rate. Drinking alcohol faster than the liver can metabolise it will cause the blood alcohol concentration (BAC) to rise, and the person will show signs of intoxication. If this continued unchecked, it could be fatal.

How intoxicated, or drunk, a person appears depends on a range of factors:

- Sex – women are more affected by alcohol than men. They have more fat and less water in their bodies, and are generally smaller, which gives less volume to dilute the alcohol.
- Size – smaller people are more affected by alcohol. Smaller people have less volume in which to dilute the alcohol.
- Food – a person drinking on an empty stomach will be more affected by alcohol than a person who has eaten. The food slows down the rate at which the alcohol enters the bloodstream.
- General health – a person's general health can influence how the alcohol will affect them. Certain medication should not be taken with alcohol.
- Type of drink – a person drinking fizzy alcoholic drinks, such as sparkling wine and stronger drinks like spirits, may appear to be affected sooner, as these tend to be absorbed more quickly.
- Tolerance – a person who only drinks occasionally will appear to be more affected than a regular drinker. This is because they have a low tolerance to alcohol. As with any drug, a person who drinks alcohol regularly will develop a certain tolerance to it. This doesn't mean that they become immune to alcohol, but only that it takes more alcohol before it appears that they are affected.
- Age – younger people are more affected by alcohol because they are still growing: even though a young person has reached their adult height, their internal organs may not be fully developed and are therefore more susceptible to damage. Older people are more affected because they have a larger proportion of fat to water, and the rate at which alcohol is broken down slows as we age.

Did you know?

41% of men and 34% of women exceed recommended daily limits (Scottish Health Survey 2011).

Misconceptions

There are various myths, or misconceptions, about how to sober a person up:

Drinking coffee, cold showers, fresh air	Trying to sober up a drunken person by giving them large amounts of coffee is not a good idea. Coffee can even worsen the effect because it contains caffeine, a stimulant, which speeds up the body so that more alcohol is carried to the brain. Similarly, taking a cold shower or getting some fresh air may make the person feel less sleepy, but does not affect the amount of alcohol in the blood.
Drinking water	Drinking water will offset some of the dehydrating effects of alcohol. This might prevent a person from having such a sore head in the morning, but it won't affect the amount of alcohol they've drunk.
Eating something	Eating before and during drinking will slow down the rate at which alcohol gets into the bloodstream. Eating after drinking will make no difference.
A good night's sleep	Sleeping does not make the liver process the alcohol out of your body any quicker. In fact, alcohol – even in very small amounts – disturbs normal sleep patterns.
Being sick	Being sick only gets rid of the alcohol that is still in the stomach. It does not affect the amount that has already been absorbed into the blood.

Units of alcohol

Being able to work out the units of alcohol in a drink gives a simple way to compare the amount of alcohol contained in one drink with another. It also allows a person to compare their drinking with recommended low-risk guidelines. Understanding the number of units per drink also helps in calculating approximately how long it might take all the alcohol to be broken down (which may not be until the following day).

In Britain, a unit is 10ml of pure alcohol (8 grams of alcohol). However, we couldn't drink alcohol in this form. So a drink contains a certain concentration of alcohol, or alcohol by volume (ABV), along with water, flavourings and

colourings. The simple idea that one drink – for example, a glass of wine, a sherry, a nip or a half pint of beer or cider – equals one unit was introduced some time ago, when people generally drank standard-strength beers and lower-strength wines. Things are very different today. For instance, the strength of beer ranges from low-alcohol beer at about 1% ABV to standard beer of about 4% ABV, through to super-strength beers of around 8% ABV.

In order to find out the exact number of units in a drink, you need to do a simple calculation. First multiply the volume of the drink in millilitres by the ABV, and then divide by 1000.

Formula	size (ml) × strength (ABV) ÷ 1000 = units
Example	750ml bottle of wine at 13% ABV means (750 × 13) ÷ 1000 = 9.75 units

How much is too much?

The Royal College of Physicians has drawn up weekly guidelines for units:

	Women	Men
Low risk	up to 14	up to 21
Increased danger	14–35	21–49
Dangerous	over 35	over 49

When these guidelines came out, people tended to 'save' their units and drink them all in one session of 'binge drinking'. As this is not a healthy or safe way of drinking, in 1995 a government report suggested that weekly limits should be revised to daily limits.

The report by the Department of Health suggested that men who drink three to four units a day (but not more) and women who drink two to three units per day (but not more) don't face a significant health risk. There should also be at least two alcohol-free days each week.

	Women	Men
Units per day (two alcohol-free days a week)	2–3 units per day	3–4 units per day

Don't forget that an average glass of wine in a pub (250ml at 13% ABV) and a pint of premium lager at 5% ABV are each equivalent to around three units. Consistently drinking more than this in one day is not advisable because of the increased health risk.

Children and young people

For younger people, drinking alcohol can be problematic not only because they are smaller, which means they will have a higher concentration of alcohol in the blood than adults, but also because they are just beginning to drink alcohol, and so will have lower tolerance: even a small amount of alcohol may have a large effect. This means that they can reach the level of acute alcohol poisoning – which can be fatal – with far less alcohol than an adult who drinks regularly.

Drinking too much alcohol at an early age can affect brain and bone development. This damage can be irreversible. An alcohol-free childhood is best. We know that the earlier a person starts drinking, the higher the risk that they will experience alcohol-related problems later in life.

Scottish schoolchildren are asked to take part in the biennial Scottish Schools Adolescent Lifestyle and Substance Use Survey (SALSUS). In the 2013 survey, 70% of 15-year-olds said they had had an alcoholic drink, along with 32% of 13-year-olds. Those who had drunk alcohol were asked if they had experienced specific outcomes, ranging from vomiting to being admitted to hospital. The effects of drinking are shown in the table on page 63.

Where do children purchase alcohol?

In the 2013 SALSUS survey, the majority of 13- and 15-year-olds who had drank alcohol said they didn't buy it – they got it from friends, relatives or took it from home (with or without permission). For licensed premises this means that you should be extra vigilant about adults who are acting as an agent for underagers (see page 94). Children's sources for acquiring alcohol are shown in the table on page 63.[1]

What will young people try to buy?

In 2006 Alcohol Focus Scotland carried out a study of refusals books from a range of premises throughout Scotland over a five-month period. The most popular purchases were vodka and lager, with tonic wine and cider next. A 2013 survey of alcohol brands consumed by under-18's in contact with drug and alcohol services in England and Wales, carried out by Alcohol Concern, showed that the most popular were Fosters beer, generic or own-brand

---

1 The graph at the top of the opposite page shows the effects of drinking experienced by 15-year-olds at least once in a one year period. The graph at the bottom shows sources for 15-year-olds who said they had drunk alcohol. Percentages of both graphs add up to more than 100% because 15-year-olds were given a list of options and asked to pick all that apply. Source: SALSUS, 2013 report.

vodka, Smirnoff vodka, Frosty Jack's cider and Glen's vodka. It suggests that young people are most influenced by a combination of price, strength and awareness of product marketing.[2]

Effects of alcohol reported by 15-year-olds

	%	
☺☺☺☺☺☺☺☺☺☺	33%	had an argument
☺☺☺☺☺☺☺☺☺	28%	sent a text/email that you wished you hadn't
☺☺☺☺☺	15%	posted on social media and wished you hadn't
☺☺☺☺☺	15%	been in trouble with police
☺☺☺☺☺	14%	tried drugs
☺☺☺☺	13%	ended up in a situation where they felt threatened/unsafe
☺☺☺☺	13%	had a fight
☺☺	7%	stayed off school
☺	4%	been to hospital

0% 25% 50% 75% 100%

Where do 15-year-olds get alcohol?

	%	
☺☺☺☺☺☺☺☺☺☺☺☺☺☺	46%	friend
☺☺☺☺☺☺☺☺☺☺☺	34%	relative
☺☺☺☺☺☺☺	25%	home (either with or without permission)
☺☺☺	8%	shop
☺☺	5%	off-licence
☺	2%	supermarket
☺	2%	pub or bar
☾	1%	stolen from an off-licence/shop/supermarket
☾	1%	club or disco

0% 25% 50% 75% 100%

2 Source: *Alcohol brands consumed by under-18s in contact with young people's drug and alcohol services*, Alcohol Concern, 2013

It is a requirement that you train your staff, so make sure your training includes the very good reasons why the legal age to purchase alcohol has been set at 18. They also need to know what young people try to buy. It's up to you and your staff to enforce the law. Information on how to deal with refusal of service is covered in Part 4 of this book.

Drink driving, accidents and crime

Drinking and driving

Since December 2014, the legal limit for driving in Scotland is 50 milligrams of alcohol in 100 millilitres of blood. This brings Scotland into line with many European countries. Impairment of driving ability actually occurs at less than this. It would be extremely difficult to identify how many drinks it will take for someone to reach the legal limit, because it is dependent on a number of factors such as sex, size, food, etc. The only safe advice is to consume no alcohol before driving.

Whilst there are a number of offences under the Licensing (Scotland) Act 2005 related to drunkenness, there is no legal definition of 'drunk'. It is a subjective judgement based on a person's behaviour. In contrast, drink driving offences are based on an objective measure of the concentration of alcohol in the blood, or BAC (blood alcohol content).

Although it is not a legal responsibility for you to prevent drink driving, there are good reasons for discouraging it, for the safety of your customers and the community. If you work in on-licence premises, you can do the following to encourage customers not to drink and drive:

Serve soft drinks	▪ Display soft drinks and non-alcoholic alternatives together where they can be clearly seen. ▪ Try stocking some of the more interesting alternatives to alcohol that are now available. ▪ Know the difference between low-alcohol and non-alcoholic drinks (see section on the Trade Descriptions Act in Part 2).
Serve food	▪ This slows down the rate of alcohol entering the bloodstream. It also gives people something to do other than drink, and makes good business sense. It works particularly well now that people can no longer smoke in enclosed spaces.
Inform and educate your customers	▪ Display drink drive materials such as posters or drinks mats and bar towels. The car park is a particularly effective place to put up a drink drive message. ▪ Display phone numbers for taxi firms, or offer to call taxis for customers.

A few words of caution: don't exceed your authority. If someone is clearly over the limit and you realise they're intending to drive, you could offer to call them a taxi, but you cannot take their keys from them unless they choose to hand them over. This could be seen as theft. Don't try to physically restrain a person, as this could be seen as assault. You may feel it's friendly to offer to drive someone home, but if you have an accident you could face insurance problems. Instead, you can phone the police anonymously on Crimestoppers: 0800 555 111. Your house policy should include your policy on drink drivers.

Costs to Scotland of alcohol misuse

Alcohol affects everyone in Scotland, whether we drink alcohol or not. Alcohol misuse was estimated to cost Scotland £3.56 billion in 2007. This equates to £900 per year for every adult living in Scotland.
▪ healthcare-related costs: £267.8 million
▪ social care costs: £230.5 million
▪ crime costs: £727.1 million
▪ costs to the productivity of the Scottish economy: £865.7 million
▪ human cost in terms of suffering caused by premature deaths: £1.46 billion[3]

3 *The Societal Cost of Alcohol Misuse in Scotland for 2007*, York Health Economics Consortium, University of York, 2010

The social consequences

Families and children

- Children whose parents drink at problematic levels have been found to have higher levels of behavioural difficulty, school-related problems and emotional disturbance.[4] It is estimated that up to 51,000 children in Scotland are living with a parent who has an alcohol problem.
- In the UK a disproportionately large number of calls to Childline from children concerned about a significant other's (eg parent, carer) drinking, came from Scotland.[5]
- One in three divorce petitions in the UK cites excessive drinking by a partner as a contributory factor.[6]

Crime and assaults

Drunkenness has a high association with some common crimes. People who are drunk:

- are more likely to assault someone or be assaulted (particularly young men)
- have a higher likelihood of being involved in domestic violence, such as assaulting their partner or their children.

97% of respondents to the Scottish Crime and Justice Survey 2009/10 considered alcohol abuse in Scotland to be a big problem. In 62% of violent crimes, the attacker was believed to be under the influence of alcohol. Almost half of young victims (aged 16–24) were under the influence of alcohol themselves. Half of all prisoners were drunk at the time of their offence, rising to 77% of young offenders.[7]

70% of all assaults handled by emergency departments are alcohol-related.[8]

Fire

Alcohol or drugs were a factor in at least one in six accidental house fires in Scotland in 2010/11. They were suspected to have contributed to 835 of the 5,254 accidental fires, and caused 11 deaths. The most common causes of fires where alcohol is a contributory factor involve the careless use of cigarettes, lighters and matches, or misuse of chip pans and cooking appliances while making food.

---

4 *Looking Beyond Risk: Parental Substance Misuse: Scoping Study*, Scottish Executive, 2006
5 *Untold damage: Children's accounts of living with harmful parental drinking*, Scottish Health Action on Alcohol Problems (SHAAP)/Childline, 2009
6 *Alcohol Harm Reduction project: Interim Analytical Report*, Prime Minister's Strategy Unit, 2003
7 *Alcohol Statistics Scotland 2011*, Information Statistics Division (ISD) Scotland, NHS Scotland
8 Scottish Emergency Department Alcohol Audit, 2006

Accident and emergency

Unfortunately alcohol is involved in many more accidents, injuries and fatalities than we commonly realise. It is the police and medical staff who have to cope with the results. The peak time for accidents and injuries falls just after the majority of licensed premises close. The high points are Friday and Saturday nights between midnight and 04.00. Pubs tend to close at 23.00 or midnight, and clubs between 01.00 and 03.00. There are approximately 400 alcohol-related deaths from home accidents annually in the UK.[9]

It's worth considering what happens to people found by the police to be 'drunk and incapable' (which is actually an offence). They're either taken to hospital to be checked and then kept in the police cells where someone can keep an eye on them, or taken to an alcohol detoxification centre, where they will be supervised.

Drunk and incapable people are detained because they pose a risk to themselves and others. It is with good reason that the laws on drunkenness exist. It's up to you and your staff to enforce them.

The law gives you and your staff a legal responsibility to decide whether to continue to sell alcohol or to refuse. Customers, particularly those who have already been drinking, may not be in the best position to judge for themselves. If you work in an off-sales premises, you don't know when or where a customer is going to consume the alcohol being purchased, but it is likely that a drunk person is buying more alcohol to consume immediately.

Health

Both health professionals and the government are concerned about the risks to health associated with drinking large quantities of alcohol. In 2011 there were 1,247 deaths involving alcohol as an 'underlying' or 'contributory' factor. That's 24 people dying every week from alcohol.

Alcohol problems take many different forms, including:
- drinking above low-risk limits
- binge drinking
- needing a drink to relax
- alcohol dependency.

Alcohol in certain situations can be particularly risky, such as when driving or during pregnancy.

Health threats

There are many ways in which alcohol can put health at risk. Short-term health problems, associated with single sessions of drunkenness, ie binge drinking, include:

- hangover (headache, nausea, etc)
- temporary memory loss
- accidents and injuries
- disturbed sleep patterns
- increased risk of stroke and heart problems
- high blood pressure
- impotence
- acute alcohol poisoning
- unwanted and/or unprotected sex, and associated risk of pregnancy and sexually transmitted infections.

Pregnancy

Pregnant women or women trying to conceive should avoid drinking alcohol. Although researchers don't know exactly how much alcohol is safe to drink when pregnant, we do know that the risk of damage to the unborn baby increases the more alcohol is consumed. Binge drinking is particularly harmful. Heavy drinking is associated with miscarriage, and sometimes with serious effects on a baby's development including premature birth, facial deformity, hearing and vision problems, hyperactivity, memory, and attention and judgement problems.

Liver problems

Alcohol is primarily broken down in the liver, which can damage the liver cells. Cirrhosis occurs when liver cells die, leaving scarring or distortion of the liver. It is most commonly a disease that affects people who have been drinking hazardously over a number of years. The highest rates of cirrhosis tend to be found in people in their late 40s or their 50s. However, in recent years cirrhosis rates in younger age groups have also increased. The chart on the following page gives a comparison of deaths attributed to cirrhosis of the liver in Scotland, England and Wales, and other European countries.

Deaths attributed to liver disease

In 1990, one in 100 deaths was directly attributed to alcohol. The NHS report, 'Alcohol attributable mortality and morbidity' published in 2009, showed this had risen to one in 20 deaths in less than 20 years. This rise compares very badly to our nearest neighbours – England and Wales – and to the rest of Europe. It's worth noting that Scotland has changed – we used to drink a lot less than we do now.

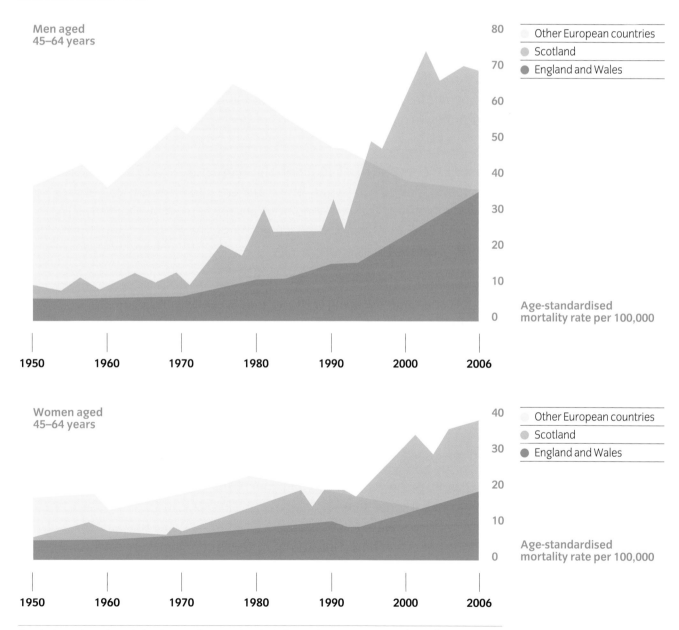

Men aged
45–64 years

Other European countries
Scotland
England and Wales

Age-standardised
mortality rate per 100,000

1950 1960 1970 1980 1990 2000 2006

Women aged
45–64 years

Other European countries
Scotland
England and Wales

Age-standardised
mortality rate per 100,000

1950 1960 1970 1980 1990 2000 2006

Graphs based on 'Liver cirrhosis mortality rates in Britain from 1950 to 2002: an analysis of routine data', *The Lancet*, Vol. 367, January 2007. Rates for England and Wales (to 2004) and Scotland (to 2006) subsequently updated by Professor David Leon and the General Registrar for Scotland.

Cancer

Alcohol is an established risk factor for the development of cancer. Drinking alcohol increases the risk of developing cancer of the breast, mouth, throat, larynx (voice box), oesophagus, bowel and liver. Smoking and drinking together increases the cancer risk even more.

Blood pressure and heart problems

There is an established link between high blood pressure and alcohol intake. Regular heavy drinking, and particularly binge drinking, is associated with raised blood pressure, which puts the individual at risk of a stroke. A bout of heavy drinking is one of the most common causes of strokes in young people. Heavy drinking can result in heart damage. The heart muscle can enlarge and become less efficient at its job of pumping blood around the body, contributing to cardiomyopathy and congestive heart failure.

Diabetes and pancreatitis

Alcohol is the second most common cause of acute pancreatitis, and long-term heavy drinking can cause chronic pancreatitis. This can lead to diabetes. The vast majority of diabetic conditions are not caused by heavy drinking – however, anyone diagnosed as diabetic has to take into account the high number of calories in alcoholic drinks.

Gastritis and malnutrition

Alcohol can irritate the lining of the stomach. Nausea and vomiting, sometimes with blood, are not uncommon. Chronic gastritis can reduce the appetite, resulting in vitamin deficiencies.

Fertility

Both men and women can be affected. In men, excessive drinking can lower sperm count, be a factor in impotence and cause hormonal imbalances that result in testicular shrinkage and breast development. In women, heavy drinking is thought to increase the chances of miscarriage.

Brain damage and intellectual impairment

Heavy drinkers show brain shrinkage on brain scans. In addition, there are a number of brain-related illnesses associated with people who drink heavily over long periods of time. Unfortunately these conditions are on the increase.

High-risk occupations

If you work in an on-licence premises, you should be aware that you're in a high-risk occupation for cirrhosis of the liver and other diseases associated with alcohol.

Why are some occupations high-risk? Three main factors tend to increase risk:
- alcohol is easily available
- alcohol is at an affordable price
- the occupation is stressful.

Bear in mind that just because in your lifestyle you 'normally' spend a lot of time in a pub and may also socialise there, this may not be 'normal' for everyone. Licensees may have to pay higher rates of insurance because of their increased risk.

You should also consider the possible effects of alcohol misuse on your business. Staff members with an alcohol problem are likely to have periods when they are not functioning well, and also increased periods of absence. Do what you can to reduce any risks, and have in a place a policy to deal with problems, if they arise.

Some things you can do:
- make sure you run any staff social events responsibly
- train your staff to understand the risks alcohol poses to their own health
- have in place an alcohol policy that states your rules on staff drinking while at work, and how you would support someone with an alcohol problem. For more help in creating an alcohol policy, seek the guidance of a specialist agency such as Alcohol Focus Scotland.

Health and the Licensing Act

The effect of alcohol misuse on Scotland's health is huge and rapidly growing worse. The Licensing (Scotland) Act 2005 includes the licensing objective, 'protecting and improving public health'. You may want to consider the following suggestions:

On-licence	promote competitively priced non-alcoholic drinks
	encourage customers to eat as well as drink
	use smaller measures for wine and spirits
	encourage customers to space out alcoholic drinks with soft drinks
	don't allow customers to play drinking games
	limit the number of drinks that can be purchased, ie one drink per person
	avoid time limited promotions.

Off-licence	promote quality over quantity
	avoid promotions that encourage customers to buy larger amounts
	limit the amount of alcohol to be purchased.
Both on- and off-licence	display information on units of alcohol and the dangers of excessive drinking
	offer drinks with a lower alcoholic strength
	train staff on the effects of alcohol
	promote alternatives to alcohol.

What to do if a person collapses

Sometimes it may be difficult to tell whether a person is intoxicated by alcohol (or another drug) or whether they have some form of illness or disability. If the person collapses, your response should be the same:

1 Call for help immediately.
2 Call an ambulance (or ask someone to do it for you).
3 Check that their airways are clear.
4 Check if the person is breathing or not.
5 Loosen any tight clothing, especially at the neck and waist.

If the person is breathing, put them into the recovery position and stay with them until help arrives. The following page gives basic advice on opening the airway and the recovery position. This is not a substitute for training. For information on first aid courses, contact the local branch of the Red Cross (www.redcross.org.uk) or St Andrew's Ambulance Association (www.firstaid.org.uk).

If the person has not collapsed but is showing signs of intoxication or other suspicious behaviour, they need to be monitored until you can decide what action is appropriate. You or a member of staff should watch them carefully; perhaps try talking with them. Do not throw the person alone onto the street. This would be both dangerous and irresponsible.

Opening the airway

To open the airway:

1 Place your hand on the person's forehead and gently tilt the head back.

2 Lift the chin with two fingertips.

The recovery position

Lie the person on their side and support them by bending their other leg. The arms should be bent to support the head, making sure the airway remains clear.

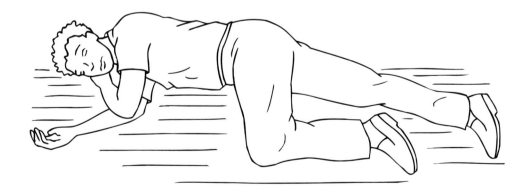

National campaigns and strategies

There are many initiatives promoting safe and responsible drinking and lots of information is available. Alcohol Focus Scotland offers a range of literature downloadable from its website: www.alcohol-focus-scotland.org.uk.

Scottish Government

The Scottish Government and NHS Health Scotland have funded a number of campaigns challenging the Scottish attitude to drinking. Information is available from www.drinksmarter.org. The Scottish Government's alcohol policy documents are available at www.scotland.gov.uk.

The latest alcohol and health statistics can be found at www.isdscotland.org.

Alcohol and Drugs Partnerships (ADPs)

In 2009, Scottish Government, CoSLA (Convention of Scottish Local Authorities) and NHS Scotland published a joint Framework for Local Partnerships on Alcohol and Drugs. This reformed the way in which local areas plan and deliver services. This Framework established 30 local Alcohol and Drug Partnerships (ADPs), which have been operational since 2009 and are mostly contiguous with local authority areas. These ADPs bring together local partners including Health Boards, local authorities, police and voluntary agencies, which are anchored in each Community Planning Partnership (CPP), and each ADP contributes to the delivery of their local CPP's Single Outcome Agreement (SOA).

They are responsible for developing local strategies and commissioning services to tackle alcohol and drugs based on an assessment of local needs; an evidence-based process for agreeing how funds should be deployed; and a clear focus on the outcomes that the investment will deliver. ADPs are well placed to assist Licensing Boards and Forums in the gathering and analysis of evidence and providing local context, in order to support the development of licensing policy and practice.

Minimum pricing

Minimum pricing is part of the Scottish Government's overall strategy to address Scotland's health. There is a clear link between consumption and price – as the price of alcohol has fallen, consumption and related harm has risen. Alcohol is 44% more affordable today than 30 years ago. There has been

increased competition between retailers, who have responded by cutting prices and offering deep discounts and promotions, with the result that alcohol, a legal drug, is available at low prices.

The most effective way of reducing consumption and harm is increasing the price of alcohol relative to income. Minimum pricing is an effective policy because it targets the drinkers causing the most harm to themselves and society, whilst having very little effect on moderate drinkers.

The Alcohol Minimum Pricing (Scotland) Bill was passed by the Scottish Parliament on 24 May 2012. This will pave the way for the introduction of a minimum unit price, expected to be 50p.

Modelling carried out by the University of Sheffield estimated that in the first year alone, introducing a 50p minimum unit price in Scotland would mean fewer deaths, fewer hospital admissions and fewer crimes. The law has not yet come into force. For more information, please see www.alcohol-focus-scotland.org.uk/campaigns/minimum-pricing.aspx.

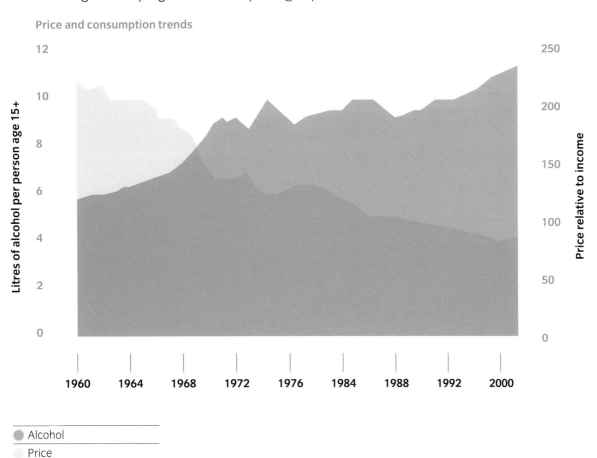

Price and consumption trends

Alcohol
Price

Source: Academy of Medical Sciences (2004) *Calling Time: the Nation's Drinking as a Major Health Issue.*

Self check

1 Name **three** types of alcohol covered by the Licensing (Scotland) Act 2005.

2 What type of drug is alcohol?

3 What are considered the low-risk weekly limits of alcohol for men and women?

4 How can you calculate what a unit of alcohol is?

5 What is the current drink driving limit?

6 Name **three** possible risks to health associated with drinking large quantities of alcohol.

7 Name **two** ways you can ensure you do not promote irresponsible drinking.

Test practice

1 Which of the following are possible consequences to an individual of excessive drinking on one occasion?

1 Increased risk of becoming a victim of crime
2 Increased risk of becoming successful
3 Death from alcohol poisoning
4 Short-term memory loss
5 Death from liver cirrhosis

a 1, 3, 4
b 1, 2, 5
c 1, 3, 5
d 2, 3, 4

2 Approximately how long will it take for the liver to begin to break down alcohol?

a 2 minutes
b 20 minutes
c 2 hours
d 20 hours

3 Which **one** of the following best describes why binge drinking is a problem?

a People enjoy themselves too much
b People spend too much money
c People are more vulnerable to accidents
d People are more likely to be tired

4 If a unit of alcohol is 10ml, which **one** of the following makes up the rest of every type of alcoholic drink?

a Water and sugar
b Caffeine and sugar
c Water and flavourings
d Caffeine and flavourings

Managing the premises and people

As a premises or personal licence holder, you have responsibilities relating directly to the type of environment you create and the way you manage it. The Licensing (Scotland) Act 2005 requires you at all times to uphold the five licensing objectives:

1 Preventing crime and disorder
2 Securing public safety
3 Preventing public nuisance
4 Protecting and improving public health
5 Protecting children from harm

This part of the book looks at ways to help you create the right environment – one that is in keeping with the licensing objectives, and one where customers have a high-quality experience and return to your premises again and again. The following information can help you fulfil your legal and social responsibilities and run a successful business.

The key aspects covered in this section are:
■ offering good customer service
■ creating the right setting
■ preventing problems and dealing with situations promptly.

Did you know?

A typical dissatisfied customer will tell six to ten people about the problem. A typical satisfied customer will tell only one or two. (Based on the National Complaints Culture Survey 2006, carried out by the National Association of Corporate Directors.)

Customer service

Good customer service means having high standards in the way you and your staff treat customers. This includes being friendly, polite, helpful and easily recognisable (eg wearing a uniform). It's not always easy to give good service, especially when you're busy, but it's important to do your best. The service that customers receive is what they remember. If it is good service, they're more likely to come back. Standards of customer service will influence the reputation of the premises; this in turn means that customers know what to expect in your premises, and encourages them to behave to the same standards.

Working in a licensed premises, you have different roles to juggle. Two of the most important are 'salesperson' and 'police officer'. Good customer service requires that you and your staff are good at both.

The 'salesperson'

Selling is an important part of serving. If you didn't sell anything, you wouldn't have a business and your staff wouldn't have jobs. Train staff on the products you sell, and listen to the customer to find out exactly what they want. Staff should display product knowledge – for example, be able to suggest alternatives if you don't have a particular brand so you don't lose a sale, or be able to offer complementary products to encourage customers to buy other things as well. For example, selling snacks, food, coffee and other non-alcoholic drinks offers customers more choice and makes them feel like they've received good service. These items often have a higher profit margin than alcoholic drinks!

The 'police officer'

The role of 'police officer', that is, the enforcer of the law, is one that everyone – from new staff to experienced managers – generally feels less confident about. Providing good service can assist you with this role. It's best practice to establish a good relationship from the beginning. Make eye contact and welcome everyone who comes into the premises. By showing that you notice what happens, you put out the message that you're in control. Providing good service each time you come into contact with the customer reinforces this image. It also gives the impression that you and your staff are nice people who deserve respect. This means that people are more likely to be better behaved, and your premises are less likely to be seen as a soft option for people wanting to carry out illegal activities such as underage drinking or theft. It is also extremely important that there is communication between staff, and that there are plans for what to do in difficult or conflict situations (an 'escalation policy') so that everyone works together.

The right setting

Housekeeping

The things that annoy all customers seem to revolve around standards of basic cleanliness and housekeeping. Customers form an impression of your premises almost immediately when they come through the door (or even before – if the exterior is dirty and poorly maintained, they may not bother coming in at all).

You need to ensure that the premises are in a good state of repair and that tidiness and cleanliness of the premises are maintained throughout the day. Other things that influence your customers are lighting, layout, decor, music, point-of-sale materials, other customers and staff – especially how quickly the staff notice them. The standards set by your premises will, to a large extent, determine the type of customers that you attract and their standards of behaviour. If the counter is dirty or cluttered and the service poor, then it seems as if no-one will care about standards of behaviour either.

Influencing behaviour

The relationship between alcohol and behaviour, especially conflict, is not a simple one. One of the first effects of alcohol is to reduce inhibitions. If someone has been drinking and they become angry, they're less likely to be inhibited about what they say and do than they normally would be. We can't say that alcohol causes conflict; however, research carried out in on-licence premises suggests that conflict is more common where there is drunkenness.

Drinking behaviour depends on three different factors:

Alcohol	Amount of alcohol consumed on the occasion.
Person	Characteristics of the person drinking and that person's state of mind.
Environment	Layout, atmosphere and rules of the establishment where the person is.

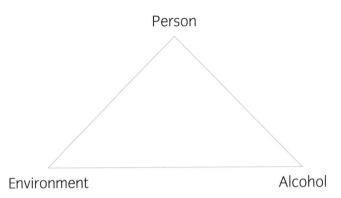

Person

Environment   Alcohol

Changing any one of these factors will alter drinking behaviour. For example, a person's behaviour when sitting at home watching TV is likely to be very different from that same person's behaviour at a party or nightclub, where there are lots of people, loud music and movement, even if exactly the same amount of alcohol is consumed in both circumstances.

Staff in on-licence premises can influence the amount and type of alcohol customers consume – we looked at this in Part 3. All licensed premises control their environment.

Music
You may be providing music to attract customers or to influence them in some way. The type of music played and how loud it is can affect the behaviour of your customers. There have been some experiments with different types and speeds of music. In shops, playing classical music seems to reduce shoplifting. In bars, playing happy music at the end of the night can mean customers leave in a good mood.

It's good practice to have a music policy, with different sorts of music for different times. The music can help to calm things down or liven things up as needed.

Problem customers
Your customers also have an effect on the atmosphere. Like tends to attract like, eg young people are likely to attract other young people, large groups attract other large groups and drunkenness attracts others who wish to behave in a rowdy manner. The same applies with the other 'problem groups', particularly in on-licence premises, such as people selling stolen goods and especially drug takers and dealers. It's much easier to prevent any sort of problem by taking action in the early stages, rather than trying to cure the problem later.

You must ensure you assess the risks in your premises, taking into account your customers and their likely behaviour. You should have policies and plans in place to prevent and manage situations.

Tips for premises

Layout

We know that customers are going to move to certain areas. Most on-licence customers will visit the bar and inevitably also the toilets. Off-licence customers will browse the shelves and come to the counter to pay. All customers will use the doors in or out of the premises. If space is restricted in these areas, jostling among customers can easily lead to frustration and perhaps conflict. To avoid this, it is important to keep access to these areas as clear as possible.

You may also wish to consider ensuring good access for staff – ie providing ways to get out from behind the bar/till point quickly to calm things down before trouble can start.

The layout can also affect the way that people are likely to behave. For instance, in on-licence premises there is evidence to suggest that vertical drinking (ie where people stand) promotes more rapid drinking than when people are seated. Standing areas encourage social interaction, but they allow trouble to spread more quickly – you need to decide what sort of atmosphere you're trying to create and manage any risks associated with it.

Noise control

Complaints about noise can lead to a review of your licence under the licensing objective 'preventing public nuisance'. On-licence premises in residential areas especially need to consider the effects any noise from the premises could have on neighbours, particularly if you have a beer garden or external smoking area. Note that 'public nuisance' also includes mess, disturbance or light pollution, eg from illuminated signage. Your local Environmental Health Department can advise you on appropriate measures to avoid problems.

Families

Family-friendly premises are thought to reduce problems. Children of all ages can enter off-licence premises, and on-licence premises 'opt in' to having children through their operating plan. However, one of the principal objectives of the legislation is to protect children from harm, so you must ensure that your premises are a suitable environment. This should include standards for acceptable language and behaviour of adults.

Food

For on-licence premises, offering food has the added advantage of providing a way of making money while allowing customers to do something other than drink. Customers who begin by eating are much less likely to get drunk. The availability of food (especially full meals) has been associated with reduced risk of aggression in bars.

Entertainment and games in on-licence premises

The type of entertainment you provide is also important in determining the type of customer you're likely to attract. If alcohol is the only 'entertainment', people can drink too much too quickly, which generally leads to problems. However, if the entertainment encourages a lot of competition between customers, this can also lead to problems.

There is evidence to suggest that providing games such as darts, pool tables or even quizzes will lead to customers drinking more slowly but staying longer. Overall this doesn't mean that customers spend less (evidence suggests that they actually spend more), but because they drink more slowly, they're less likely to become drunk. However, because there is more interaction between people in the games areas, there is an increased likelihood of conflict. Careful monitoring of all areas, especially those where games are played, is essential.

In summary, premises that have high standards of customer service, of housekeeping and of customer behaviour are more likely to have a good atmosphere and prevent problems.

People skills

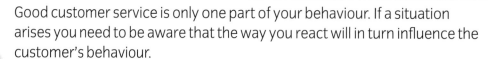

Good customer service is only one part of your behaviour. If a situation arises you need to be aware that the way you react will in turn influence the customer's behaviour.

Some people think it's okay to manage a situation using loud threats and even physical force. They allow their own aggression to take over. Most evidence suggests that this is more likely to provoke violence than to prevent it.

If you take a loud and overly forceful approach it creates a disturbance and is likely to upset other customers and give a bad impression of your premises. It is much better to try to resolve the problem using good people skills to create a win-win situation – one where the customer leaves without a grievance and the situation has been resolved without threats or violence.

Managing aggression

The table on the next page shows some of the characteristics of three types of behaviour: aggressive, assertive and passive. Ideally you and your staff should aim to be assertive when handling an incident.

It's very important that the person dealing with an incident – whether it's you or your staff – keeps calm. To do this, you must be aware of your own aggression and able to keep it under control.

What happens when someone gets angry? As the anger grows, the body starts to react physically. You may feel you're losing control, and are likely to show the signs in the 'aggressive' list in the table. This is mainly due to the hormone adrenaline. When you are particularly upset or feel threatened, the body reacts in what is known as the 'fight or flight' response. If you can remain calm and assertive, you can defuse anger and aggression in others.

Do	<ul><li>be assertive</li><li>be aware of your body language; appear to remain in control</li><li>speak slowly and evenly – if you appear calm, this will have a calming effect</li><li>respect personal space</li><li>position yourself where you feel safe, eg behind the counter, or stand slightly to one side and not directly facing the other person.</li></ul>
Don't	<ul><li>get angry – this will increase the risk of conflict</li><li>shout or point, as this can be seen as aggression</li><li>show fear or passivity.</li></ul>

Removing triggers

Good service can remove some of the 'triggers' that can lead to frustration and anger. Common examples of poor customer service include:

- ignoring customers
- not serving people in turn
- being rude or unhelpful
- having dirty or messy premises
- leaving stuff lying around and not tidied away – eg empty boxes on shelves in off-sales.

Body language

	Aggressive	Assertive	Passive
Posture	Leaning forward, rigid	Upright/straight	Shrinking
Head	Chin jutting out	Firm, not rigid	Head down
Eyes	Strongly focused, staring, often piercing or glaring eye contact	Good regular eye contact	Glancing away or downwards, little eye contact
Face	Set or firm, red (or very white)	Expression fits the words	Smiling even when upset
Voice	Loud, emphatic, speaking quickly, threats	Well modulated to fit content	Hesitant or soft, trailing off at ends of words or sentences, wavering
Arms/hands	Hands on hips, fists, sharp gestures, fingers pointing, jabbing	Relaxed, moving easily, open palms	Aimless, fidgeting
Movement/ walking	Slow and pounding or fast and deliberate	Measured pace suited to the situation	Slow and hesitant or fast and jerky
In general	Heart beating faster, breathing rapidly		

As discussed earlier, the service tends to set the tone. Therefore, if different staff treat customers in different ways, customers will not know what standards are expected of them. This can lead to arguments and conflict between customers and with staff, so it's important that there is a consistent standard throughout the premises. This applies to the physical surroundings as well as to the behaviour of staff.

The frustration caused by poor customer service may build up until the customer eventually 'explodes'. Remember that something may have upset the customer before they come into your premises – another good reason to try and pay attention to each person as they come in. The graph below shows that once someone is already frustrated or annoyed, it won't take much to trigger them into what the graph calls a 'crisis phase'. This could lead to a verbal or even physical assault on you, your staff or other customers.

The assault cycle

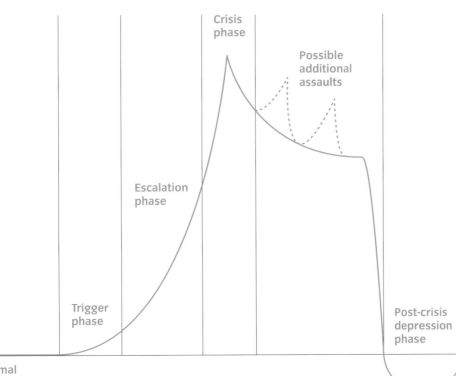

Crisis phase

Possible additional assaults

Escalation phase

Trigger phase

Post-crisis depression phase

Normal behaviour

It's better to try to calm people in the early stages. An example of this would be dealing with a customer complaint immediately and to their satisfaction. If people get to the top of the escalation phase or into the crisis phase, they are much more difficult to control and trouble is more likely.

People may remain in a 'heightened' state for several hours after an aggressive outburst, and during this period it is easy to 'trigger' them into repeated outbursts. This is something that servers who are dealing with customers at the end of the evening need to take into account.

Dealing with complaints

A complaint is an opportunity to turn a dissatisfied customer into a satisfied one. It's a fact of life that dissatisfied customers tend to be very vocal. They often tell their friends about their bad experience, or make a comment via the internet, putting off potential customers. Every member of the team should know how to handle complaints, as a badly handled complaint can escalate into an argument or 'verbal conflict'. The dos and don'ts on the following page give the basics.

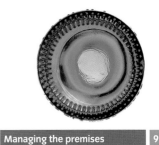

Do	<ul><li>listen to the customer without interrupting</li><li>try to acknowledge their point of view – you don't have to agree with them, just try to show that you understand, eg 'I can see how that has upset you'</li><li>show you're taking the complaint seriously by listening and questioning them to clarify matters</li><li>paraphrase or repeat the complaint back to the person: 'So, you're saying that…', which shows you have understood the issue</li><li>take action. Tell them what you intend to do.</li></ul>
Don't	<ul><li>take the complaint personally</li><li>let yourself become angry</li><li>get into arguments with customers</li><li>blame colleagues, which looks unprofessional and shows a weakness in the staff team</li><li>try to justify your actions or make complicated excuses – they don't want to know why the problem happened, just what you are going to do about it</li><li>make jokes at the customer's expense.</li></ul>
You may need to	<ul><li>apologise even if it is not your fault, eg 'I'm sorry that there's been a misunderstanding here'</li><li>let the customer have the last word.</li></ul>

Managing busy situations

It's easy for service standards to change if the premises are quiet or busy. For example, some servers are more likely to chat amongst themselves or do other tasks when there are few customers. This may mean those customers feel ignored. Equally, some servers will find it difficult to pay attention to anything other than the customer in front of them when it is busy. As a manager you need to plan levels of staff and staff duties to meet the needs of quieter and busier occasions. For example, on a really busy night, some staff may only serve customers whilst other staff have the job of clearing tables, stacking shelves and monitoring customers.

Refusing service

Refusing service is not easy and creates a situation where there is potential for conflict. All of the following tips will help:

- Always be polite. It's a good idea to start with an apology, eg 'I'm sorry but…'
- Try to give a reason that stresses your legal or professional responsibilities, eg 'It's against the law to serve you without proof of age. Otherwise I could be fined or lose my job.'
- Try to follow your refusal with some kind of positive. If this is also a question, it helps to provide a distraction, eg 'Can I get you anything else?'
- Be assertive.

Remember you are just refusing service and not rejecting the person!

As mentioned on page 29, it's good practice in both on-licence and off-licence premises to keep a refusals book. This is a record of who you have refused to serve and why. The record should give the date and time, plus a brief description of the person refused and the reason for the refusal. It is also useful to note which products the person was attempting to buy. The refusals book shows you are abiding by the laws. It also helps to identify any patterns, which will help you plan staff resources, and extra training if required, accordingly.

Refusing underagers

What would make you suspect that someone is underage? The person may look young, or may be behaving suspiciously – for example, appearing nervous or overconfident. They may be part of a group, with only one coming to the counter or others waiting outside. The type of drinks they're trying to buy may also be an indication, eg high-strength ciders, vodka, flavoured alcoholic beverages (alcopops), or products with a high alcohol and caffeine content. They may want to buy two half-bottles or pay with lots of small change, or with different batches of money.

Deterring underagers

The most effective way of preventing underage sales is to operate in a way that deters young people from attempting to buy alcohol.

Premises must have a 'Challenge 25' policy in place. This means that every person who appears to be under 25 is asked for proof that he or she is aged 18 or over. All staff need to be vigilant and trained to ask every person who appears to be under 25 for proof of age, and must not serve the person unless appropriate proof is shown.

It is good practice to:

- Display signage informing customers what proof of age will be accepted.
- Regularly review your system, and remind your staff of their responsibilities. Training them once is not enough!

Some companies do 'integrity testing', where they send a young-looking adult in to try and buy alcohol and check that staff ask for proof of age. Obviously you cannot ask someone who is under 18 to do this, as this would be illegal.

Tips for off-licence premises

In off-sales premises, groups of young people hanging around and drinking nearby may lead some people to assume that because they're in the vicinity of your premises they are purchasing the alcohol there. To help prevent this you can try to ensure that you distinguish purchases from your shop, for example by having your shop name on price tickets on every product you sell. You may wish to consider installing security lights which will normally put youngsters off hanging around outside your premises. Remember that common sources of alcohol for underagers are friends, relatives or their home. Having CCTV that can be used to show who is purchasing alcohol may be of use.

Requesting proof of age

How can you request proof of age without causing conflict?

- Make sure that you and your staff are clear and confident about acceptable forms of proof of age.
- Look carefully at the birth date on the proof of age: does it prove that they are over 18?
- Treat the person with some respect. Even if they are underage and cannot buy alcohol, they are still a potential customer for other products and for the future.
- Be polite and professional, and try not to embarrass the person. Speak to them quietly and evenly, creating as little disturbance as possible.
- If in doubt, don't sell!

Remember test purchasing is legal in Scotland. As mentioned on page 30, this is where the police send an underage person (usually a 16-year-old) into premises to try to buy alcohol. If you fail a test purchase, ie if you sell them alcohol, then you could be charged, and in such cases licences are commonly suspended for a period of time.

Refusing suspected agents

If under-18s cannot purchase alcohol themselves, they will often get a friend or other adult who is 18 or over to buy it for them. This is known as 'acting as an agent' or 'proxy purchase', and is an offence. You have a responsibility to ensure that you do not sell alcohol to an agent.

Signs to look out for (both on- and off-sales):
- if the adult is known or a regular customer and they buy something they don't normally buy or something in addition to their usual order
- a group of young people gathered outside the shop, or in a quiet corner of the bar or beer garden.

Signs to look out for (off-sales only):
- an adult asking for the same order that has recently been refused to a young person
- an adult asking to pay separately for part of the order (especially high-risk drinks, such as strong ciders, fortified wines or alcopops)
- an adult buying multiples of half or quarter bottles
- an adult making repeat visits in a single evening.

In this situation it is best to:
- politely challenge the person
- explain the legal position, ie that if the drinks are for underage people, then the server cannot sell them as the adult would be committing the offence of 'acting as an agent'
- speak to the youngsters and ask them to disperse, or if they're causing a public nuisance, you may wish to call the police and ask them to move the group on.

If the adult denies acting as an agent you may want to watch what the adult does with the drinks. On-licence premises will have to take the drinks from the under-18s, and you could also ask them and the adult to leave; off-licence premises may wish to phone the police and report the adult.

Refusing suspected drunken people

It is an offence to allow a breach of the peace, drunkenness or other disorderly conduct; it is an offence to sell alcohol to a drunken person and it is also an offence for a drunken person to enter or remain on licensed premises. As we have seen already, it is up to the server to decide if someone is drunk.

Most servers agree that if a person is having trouble with their speech or movement, it is likely they are drunk. Remember: you always have the right

to refuse service and to ask a person to leave. You may need to approach the person and speak with them to help determine your initial suspicions. This gives you the chance to detect the smell of alcohol which is often present when a person is drunk.

Best practice for refusing service to a drunken person is to:
- Approach the person as soon as possible. If possible, meet them at the door and speak with them. If they do come in, it may be more difficult to persuade them to leave.
- Speak slowly and clearly. Remember that the effect of the alcohol on a drunken person will lessen their ability to think and even to understand.
- Keep your voice neutral. Never raise your voice, shout, make loud threats or show any other signs of aggression or anger. This is likely to provoke an angry response in the drunken person and make the situation more difficult to deal with.
- Choose your words carefully. It is better to say something like 'I think you've had (a little) too much to drink', rather than, 'You're drunk'.
- Use the broken record technique. That is, keep repeating the same or similar statements, eg 'I'm sorry, I can't serve you … I could lose my job.'

Remember the alcohol means the person is less in control of their emotions, judgement and inhibitions than usual. Their mood can change very quickly, possibly to anger or even to violence.

If you have a well-known customer who is regularly drunk, as part of your role as 'friend', it may be helpful if you speak to them when they come in sober (not when they are drunk), and let them know that you are concerned for their well-being. If their (bad) behaviour is causing you concern, you need to explain the effect that their behaviour is having on you. You also need to explain what changes you require them to make if they are to continue to be allowed on your premises. You may find it helpful to refer the person to a specialist agency. For more information, see www.alcohol-focus-scotland. org.uk/alcohol-information/find-an-alcohol-service.aspx.

Closing time

This is the time in the evening when you have to refuse service to everyone. To make matters more difficult, your customers are probably at their most uninhibited (they've had all evening to drink alcohol) and after a long, busy evening, you and your staff are probably tired and not at your best. It's not surprising that a lot of incidents happen at this time.

At closing time you shouldn't treat your customers any differently from at any other time. You need to maintain the good relationship that you have built up with them throughout the evening. Remember, if you treat your customers with politeness and respect, that's what you're more likely to get in return. The following closing time dos and don'ts may make for a better day's end.

Do	<ul><li>have clocks that show the correct time</li><li>in on-licence, call last orders in plenty of time; in off-licences, let customers know the time they have left to pay for the alcohol</li><li>have enough staff to ensure that everyone gets served before the end of licensed hours</li><li>at the end of licensed hours make it clear that you're closed, eg switch the till/bar lights off and leave the bar area</li><li>have an established routine that shows you are closed, which may include things such as switching off fruit machines or juke boxes, or in off-licenced premises, blocking off the alcohol area</li><li>in on-licence premises, clear all glasses, etc, away as soon as they're empty and remind customers quietly and politely as you go around the tables that it is reaching the end of drinking-up time</li><li>remember to thank customers as they finish their drinks/their shopping, and to wish them good night – you're a host and a salesperson as well, so you want them to come back</li><li>chase up stragglers in a friendly manner: eg 'I hope you've enjoyed your evening, but I have to ask you to finish your drinks now as the bar is closing'</li><li>have a 'dispersal policy' (see next page).</li></ul>
Don't	<ul><li>take a 'Jekyll and Hyde' approach to closing time, ie nice one minute, nasty the next</li><li>serve anyone after the end of licensed hours – this can lead to accusations of unfairness and arguments, as well as being against the law</li><li>shout at customers or use unpleasant or aggressive tactics, as this often makes customers annoyed and more determined to be awkward.</li></ul>

Dispersal policy

A dispersal policy is relevant to premises with large numbers of people leaving at the same time, such as nightclubs. It is a plan to ensure your customers exit your premises quickly and move away from the area without causing public nuisance, eg noise, litter or fights. It may include directing customers to use particular exits, calling taxis for customers, having door stewards outside helping to direct people and calming any trouble spots. Displaying information about the transport services available near to your premises can be helpful.

Situations getting out of hand

Occasionally you may face intimidation or aggression from customers. Intimidation can include verbal abuse, racial abuse, threatening behaviour, shoplifting, criminal damage and vandalism. It is important that you and your staff work as a team and everyone monitors the customers' behaviour.

Stopping trouble early

If you notice that trouble is brewing, you should do something about it. It is much easier to 'nip it in the bud' than it is to control trouble that has already broken out. This can be more difficult in off-licence premises as your customers are in the premises for a shorter period of time, giving you less time to identify any problems and decide what action to take.

Monitoring the premises

All parts of the premises should be monitored. This can be done as staff go about their usual duties, such as stacking shelves in off-licence and collecting glasses in on-licence premises. Mirrors and CCTV can also help with this. Customers generally don't like empty shelves in a shop or dirty, cluttered table tops in a bar, so if staff go about this work with a friendly attitude, people will see your monitoring as good service. This also builds up a good relationship with customers so they're more likely to listen to you if there are problems later.

In a bar or restaurant, it's easy to pass through a crowd and listen to what's going on when you're collecting glasses and wiping down table tops. And if the worst should happen and a fight or a riot (this is rare but has been known to happen) should break out, the other advantage of collecting the glasses should be fairly obvious. Broken glasses or beer bottles can become particularly nasty weapons. If conflict should ever occur at this level you're advised to get help immediately from the police by dialling 999.

Danger signals

Depending on what kind of premises you work in, danger signals to look out for can be:

- arguments becoming heated
- raised voices
- swearing
- individuals playing up to an audience or showing off, groups becoming rowdy or silly
- drunkenness
- drinking games or contests (on-licence only)
- large groups gathering together or moving through the premises
- customers looking annoyed
- sudden silence
- regulars behaving out of character
- everyone looking in the same direction
- the sound of breaking glass
- customers acting suspiciously
- customers checking for members of staff or security cameras
- groups (or families) splitting up.

Intervention at an early stage

As soon as you become aware of a situation developing, either you or another member of staff should make some kind of intervention. It is important to remember all you have learned about handling aggression:

- keep calm
- don't get angry
- be assertive, not aggressive, and ensure your voice and body language are consistent.

There are several ways to intervene:

Casual intervention	Make your presence known, eg by collecting glasses. This may be enough to quieten things down.
Consider the environment	For example, turning the music down or playing slower tracks when customers get rowdy can help to calm things down. Equally, turning the music up increases the likelihood of conflict.

Deliberate intervention	Let people know you've noticed what's going on and that it's not okay! Speak to the people involved in a calm and assertive way, and always be tactful and polite, using such phrases as 'Is everything okay?' or 'Is there a problem here?'
Distraction	Some skilful servers are able to use distraction as an intervention method – this is easier to do if you know the person a little. You could start a conversation, eg, 'Did you see the football last night?' which can be a distraction from the situation. Alternatively, you could use humour – but you must be careful never to use humour at the customer's expense, as this could make the person feel foolish and they may react angrily.

Intervention when trouble has started

Sometimes trouble has got to a very heated stage before you can get there. This makes it much more difficult to take control. In these situations it's best to:

- Try to calm and slow things down as much as possible. Remember to speak calmly and slowly and to keep your distance.
- Try to find out what the problem is. Make sure you listen and, if appropriate, follow the procedure for complaints.
- Avoid letting other customers get involved, especially if they've been drinking.

When people are in a very heated state, they are unable to think clearly. If you ask the customer to do something they may not understand what you're asking them to do.

Escalation policy

It is good practice to have an escalation policy – ie a plan of what staff should do and when they should do it if a situation begins to get out of control. Make sure all staff are aware of the premises' escalation policy. In the case of a person refusing to leave the premises, this will usually mean summoning the assistance of other staff or the security staff. Only use physical force as a very last resort, and then only to escort someone off the premises. In an emergency situation where your staff or other customers are under threat, you should dial 999 to summon the police immediately.

Reporting crime

It is best practice to report an assault to the police during or immediately after it has happened. If there has been a crime, also remember to preserve the scene. It can be tempting to try and tidy up but this could destroy vital evidence the police will need. You should also preserve any CCTV footage.

Drug prevention

As a manager or owner of a premises (licensed or not), under the Misuse of Drugs Act 1971, it is an offence to knowingly permit drugs such as cannabis and opium to be prepared or used on the premises.

Drug-assisted sexual assault

There are many reports in the press about 'drink spiking' and 'date rape' drugs, ie when a person has added something to another person's drink with the intention of committing a sexual assault on them later. Both men and women can be victims of this type of assault; often, the person knows their assailant.

There are a range of drugs used for this purpose including alcohol, eg adding an extra shot to someone's drink without them knowing. The effects of the drugs are very similar to those of excessive alcohol, and can kick in very suddenly. Please be aware that if you or a member of staff think a customer's behaviour has suddenly changed or is out of character for them, this could be the reason.

If a customer tells staff they think their drink has been spiked, staff should take the drink from them and keep it as evidence for the police. Staff should remind customers not to leave their drinks unattended – posters and leaflets are available from the police – and be vigilant for anyone they suspect may be tampering with another person's drink.

Signs of drug taking

It's unlikely that you'll actually see any drugs, but there may be tell-tale signs, particularly in areas that are not closely monitored. This includes the toilets, quiet corners and outside areas. Signs of drug-taking include:

- syringes
- pieces of blackened/burned foil or spoons
- wrapped or rolled paper (roaches or small packets) or other unusual items
- white powder on surfaces, or very clean surfaces; discarded razor blades

- cut-down plastic bottles with holes punched in them
- bank notes that have been tightly rolled or have traces of blood on them.

Syringes are dangerous. Needles may have blood on them which can carry blood-borne viruses, eg HIV or Hepatitis C. Neither you nor your staff should touch them without taking precautions:

- Use rubber gloves and tongs or tweezers.
- Put the needle into a 'sharp safe' container (available from most drug agencies). If this is not available, use a used drinks can. Insert the needle, sharp end first, into the opening, then tape to seal the can to stop the needle escaping.
- Don't put the needle (or the needle and container) into the rubbish. Store it in a safe place until you can ask the advice of your local drugs agency or local Environmental Services Department, who may be able to collect it.

A customer's behaviour may suggest they've taken drugs. As with alcohol, people are affected differently, and different drugs have different effects. Common behaviours to watch for include:

- very dilated pupils ('saucer eyes')
- excessive sniffing, dripping nose, watering or red eyes
- sudden severe cold symptoms, or any significant change in behaviour, following a visit to the toilet/garden/car park
- white marks/traces of powder round the nose
- excessive giggling, laughing at nothing, non-stop talking
- unnaturally dopey, vacant staring, sleepy euphoria
- non-stop movement, jiggling about
- excessive consumption of soft drinks
- sudden inexplicable tearfulness or fright.

Drug dealing

It's difficult to establish that someone is drug dealing. The police are the best people to ask for advice with regards to suspected drug dealing. Drugs are often small and easily hidden. But people may act in ways that are suspicious. For example, be extra careful if you notice a person sitting in a secluded place, drinking little but staying a long time, especially if:

- they also receive short visits by lots of people
- they use the telephone a lot
- they visit the toilet often and/or make frequent trips outside
- there is lots of hand or body contact with people.

The best gauge of whether a person's actions are suspicious is the experience of you and your staff of what is 'normal' for your customers.
Any behaviour that is unusual should be monitored.

Reporting the signs of drug use

Staff should know to report anything immediately so you can monitor the signs. If you're suspicious of either drug taking or dealing, you must take action. Best practice would be to contact the police. What action you take should be part of your premises' house policy. If you do nothing, you'll develop a problem that will be much more difficult to deal with later. It is very hard to get rid of a bad reputation once it's been established.

It is up to you to look at your premises to assess risks and to reduce the likelihood of problems. If you would like help in assessing your premises' drug risk and identifying the appropriate security measures, your local police will usually be able to give advice. Scottish Drugs Forum (www.sdf.org.uk) or Crew 2000 (www.crew2000.org.uk) may also be able to offer help.

For more information on drugs, including what they look like and their short-term and long-term effects, see www.knowthescore.info – or contact the police.

The police are usually able to arrange a drugs talk/training session (complete with samples and photographs). This may be an option, particularly if you can arrange to team up with the staff from neighbouring premises to provide a large group for training.

Theft and robbery (off-licence premises)

Unfortunately some people may try to steal alcohol, particularly if they don't think they can get it any other way. There are many measures that can be taken to deter theft, including installing security and surveillance equipment. For advice on this it is best to speak to a qualified expert, such as the police Crime Prevention Officer or a security company.

There are some simple measures that you can take as well:
- Always look at and greet people as they enter your premises. This serves two purposes. It welcomes the person to your premises (part of good customer service) and lets them know that you have seen them (sending a message to potential thieves that you are watching!) .
- Monitor what's going on in your shop, especially around 'high-risk' goods.
- Be careful with floor displays. Don't arrange or stack goods up too high – it's important that you can see over displays easily.

- Don't put alcoholic drinks within easy reach of the door. Keep high-risk items, such as high-strength ciders, which can be particularly attractive to young people, in an area where you can monitor them easily.

Shoplifters

Over half of the physical assaults on retail staff are linked to attempted shoplifting. You should ensure staff know what the procedures are in your store if they see a suspected shoplifter. Have a policy. This should make it clear that no-one should risk personal safety to protect property.

Cash

Cash should be kept out of sight and not allowed to build up in the till. Where possible, banking should be done by specialist security staff. It should not be done alone, and should not be done on foot or by public transport. Staff who are expected to do it should be fully trained.

Armed robbery

In the event of an extreme situation such as an armed robbery, the following dos and don'ts sum up advice from professionals.

Do	
	- exactly what you are told by the robbers
	- make a mental note to allow you to give a description to police (appearance, details of vehicles, etc) and listen carefully to identify voices and accents and to pick up the use of names of people or places
	- keep your distance (if possible)
	- give loose notes and coins – these will fill a bag more than notes that have been counted and put into neat bundles.
Don't	
	- show hostility or attempt to fight
	- argue or speak unless spoken to
	- try to apprehend or chase the offender away from the store
	- raise the alarm until it is safe to do so
	- touch or move anything when the robbers have left – the police may be able to find fingerprints or evidence.

Remember your body language. Keep movements slow and deliberate, as sudden movements may be perceived as a threat and could provoke an aggressive response. The police can provide further advice on how to handle such extreme situations.

Barring and excluding customers

When there has been a major incident or when a customer has acted in a reckless or dangerous way, it is tempting to 'bar' the person from your premises. The following dos and don'ts can be a helpful guide:

Do	
	▪ speak to the person the next time they come in – they will often feel ashamed or sorry for causing the incident, and will be much easier to discipline
	▪ think about what possible action should be taken before speaking to the customer, eg give the person a warning or bar them for a period of time
	▪ communicate with staff. Tell them what action is being taken. It's important that all staff treat the customer in the same way.
Don't	▪ bar customers 'on the spot'. If the customer is angry and they've been drinking, they will not be thinking clearly. They may feel they have nothing to lose and act in a dangerous or reckless way.

Under the Licensing (Scotland) Act 2005, if the customer was violent you will be able to request an exclusion order (see Part 1).

Best practice following an incident

If an incident has taken place on your premises, whether on-licence or off-licence, you will want to take some steps afterward. Best practice includes keeping an incident diary. This provides a record of all incidents so that causes can be identified and steps taken to prevent problems in future. The entry in the incident diary should give an accurate picture of what happened for purposes of company communication and also for passing on to any authorities that may need details. The diary should be kept in a handy place so everyone knows where to find it.

Old diaries should be filed for possible use in any legal actions. Be sure to:

- record the incident while it is still fresh in your mind
- note any details that may be required by police or for insurance purposes.

If a crime has been committed, phone the police immediately. Preserve the crime scene while awaiting the arrival of police, and also keep any CCTV evidence.

Reassurance is also important. Recognise that both the customers and the other staff may be anxious. It's best to reassure people that everything is okay and back under control.

Recognise that you've also been through a stressful situation. If possible, take a few minutes to unwind.

Working with others in the community

Pubwatch and Retail Link

Some areas operate Pubwatch schemes where a group of licensees will work together to warn each other about potential problem customers. Normally customers who cause problems in one premises are barred from all the premises in the Pubwatch. Groups meet regularly to discuss any issues and often invite a representative from the police to attend.

Retail Link works under similar principles – retailers in an area will work together to warn each other of potential problems, normally shoplifters.

Community Safety Partnership and Safer City Centre

Linking with your local Community Safety Partnership can also be a good way of helping to create better standards in your area. This group is normally police-led, and looks at measures to promote community safety. It sometimes has small amounts of funding available for measures that promote community safety. There are similar groups in towns and city centres, often known as Safer City Centre/Safer Town Centre. They normally bring together a number of schemes, such as Pubwatch and Retail Link, and may share information about known criminals, etc. They can cover such diverse things as marshals for taxi queues, responsible drinking messages or Best Bar None schemes.

Liaison with the police

It is good practice to build a working relationship with your local police. This should include reporting any low-level crime or vandalism to allow police to accurately gauge problems in the area and allocate resources accordingly. Deterring these helps to create better standards for your premises and the whole community.

Threat of terrorism and attack

Sadly, we have to accept that crowded places, such as licensed premises, may feature in the attack plans of terrorist organisations. Terrorism can come in many forms, including physical attacks and threats or hoaxes designed to frighten and intimidate.

Health and safety legislation places a legal responsibility on the owner or occupier of premises to have a duty of care for staff and visitors. Managers need to assess the risk to their premises and have appropriate policies in place, supported by staff training.

When creating your security policy, consider the following:
- details of all the protective security measures to be implemented, covering physical, information and personnel security
- instructions on how to respond to a threat (eg telephone bomb threat) or to the discovery of a suspicious item or event, including how to report it and contact the emergency services
- a search plan
- evacuation plans and details on securing your premises in the event of a full evacuation
- your business continuity plan
- a communications and media strategy which includes handling enquiries from concerned family and friends.

Specialist advice should be sought from the police – however, basic steps to identify and prevent potential attacks will already be good practice in many premises. Staff should be vigilant and watch for unusual behaviour or items out of place, both in the premises and immediately outside. Staff should be trained to look out for packages, bags or other items in odd places, carefully placed (rather than dropped) items in rubbish bins. Good housekeeping can help with this. Be aware of unusual interest shown by strangers in the premises and surrounding area. Remember that some attacks in the UK and other countries have involved vehicles outside the premises. Ensure that staff

use existing crime prevention measures, eg they don't disable the alarm on the back door so they can nip out for a cigarette.

More detailed advice and guidance is available from the Centre for Protection of National Infrastructure, www.cpni.gov.uk, and from the National Counter Terrorism Security Office, www.nactso.gov.uk.

In summary

Training your staff in people skills will help create a friendly environment and bring many benefits to your premises.

Being able to refuse service to underage people, drunken people and those who are trying to buy alcohol for under-18s, without giving offence, maintains the law and contributes to the good standards of a premises. Efficient service and paying attention to customers prevents attempted theft and potential conflict, even terrorist threats. Good overall standards and enforcing the law makes your premises more pleasant and safe for staff and customers, which will encourage them to come back.

Most conflict can be prevented or controlled by:
- friendly, efficient service
- good monitoring, both in the premises and in the area outside
- developing a good relationship with the customer
- early intervention if there will be any question about service of alcohol
- clear signs for the customer that proof of age will be required, and what forms will be acceptable
- removing or reducing any possible sources of frustration
- clear, consistent standards of behaviour for staff and customers
- using a calm, assertive approach.

Finally, in a difficult situation, whether it's refusing service, dealing with a customer complaint, preventing theft or dealing with conflict, don't expect to get it all right the first time. It takes a lot of patience and practice to perfect all the skills.

If you do manage a situation well, remember to give yourself a pat on the back. It's not easy to remain calm and patient. If you don't handle a situation well, don't despair. Try to think about what went wrong, and think about what you could do differently. Try to do better next time.

If you can try to put into practice the things covered in this guide, you will be well on your way to becoming a well-informed and more effective licence holder.

Self check

1 A customer starts shouting at you about having to queue to be served. How would you deal with it?

2 A customer comes into your premises to buy alcohol, but you think they may be underage. What would you do?

3 What would make you suspect that an adult is buying alcohol for an underage person?

4 How would you deal with this?

5 The drinking behaviour triangle shows that **three** things influence a person's behaviour. What are they?

6 Why is good customer service important?

7 What is good practice for dealing with conflict?

Test practice

1 Which **one** of the following should be avoided when dealing with a conflict situation?

   a Other staff becoming involved
   b Other customers becoming involved
   c Asking other staff to help if things seem to be getting out of hand
   d Calling the police for help if things seem to be getting out of hand

2 Which **one** of the following is best practice if staff are being threatened by a customer?

   a Phone the local police station
   b Phone the LSO to liaise with the police
   c Phone off-duty staff to come in and help
   d Phone the police on 999

3 Which of the following lists good practice that can help to reduce common problems in licensed premises?

   1 Acknowledge customers when they enter the premises
   2 Ignore customers when they enter the premises
   3 Operate a 'no proof, no sale' policy
   4 Be aggressive if a customer complains about something
   5 Wait until a young-looking customer pays for alcohol before asking them for proof of age

   a 1, 2
   b 1, 3
   c 2, 4
   d 2, 5

4 Which **one** of the following best describes how you can keep good standards of behaviour in your premises?

   a Be friendly to customers and make it clear what standards you expect of them
   b Let customers who are your friends behave as they want to
   c Be friendly to staff and write a list of standards you expect customers to keep to
   d Let staff socialise with customers so they think it's a friendly place to be

Useful resources

Useful resources

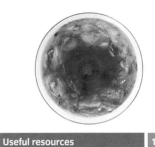

Contacts and websites

The Advertising Standards Authority (ASA) is an independent regulator that can provide useful information on advertising and promoting alcohol: www.asa.org.uk, Advertising Standards Authority, Mid City Place, 71 High Holborn, London WC1V 6QT, tel 020 7492 2222.

Alcohol Focus Scotland is Scotland's national charity working to reduce the harm caused by alcohol. It provides a range of leaflets, publications and other useful information, including details on where someone with an alcohol problem can get help: www.alcohol-focus-scotland.org.uk, Alcohol Focus Scotland, 2nd Floor, 166 Buchanan Street, Glasgow G1 2LW, tel 0141 572 6700, fax 0141 333 1606, email enquiries@alcohol-focus-scotland.org.uk.

City & Guilds is a charity established to promote education and training. It is the UK's leading provider of vocational qualifications, offering over 500 qualifications across 28 industries. It offers the Certificate for Scottish Personal Licence Holders (Off Sales) and the Certificate for Scottish Licence Holders (On Sales) as well as the Certificate for Staff Working in Scottish Licensed Premises: www.cityandguilds.com, City & Guilds, 1 Giltspur Street, London EC1A 9DD, tel 0844 543 0033, fax 020 7294 2400, email learnersupport@cityandguilds.com.

Crew 2000 provides drugs information and advice for people of all ages: www.crew2000.org.uk, tel 0131 220 3404, email admin@crew2000.org.uk.

Crimestoppers is an independent UK-wide charity working to stop crime: www.crimestoppers-uk.org. You can telephone 0800 555 111 anonymously to report problems.

Drinkline is an advice and information line for anyone who wants more information about alcohol, services that can help or simply to talk about drinking and alcohol issues: freephone 0800 7 314 314, www.drinksmarter.org.

The Environmental Health Officer at your local council can advise you on matters ranging from the Food Safety Act 1990, to the Smoking, Health and Social Care (Scotland) Act 2005 and noise reduction measures. Also usually in charge of granting Food Hygiene Certificates.

The Equality and Human Rights Commission works to eliminate discrimination, reduce inequality and protect human rights. It comprises the two bodies previously known as the Disability Rights Commission and the Equal Opportunities Commission. It provides information to disabled people on their rights and to service providers on their duties under the Disability Discrimination Act 1995. It is also a good source of information on equal opportunities and the Equal Pay Act: www.equalityhumanrights.com, Equality and Human Rights Commission, 151 West George Street, Glasgow G2 2JJ, tel 0808 800 0082, text 0808 800 0084.

The Gambling Commission is a regulatory body that can provide information on the Gambling Act 2005 and the Gambling Commission's code of practice: www.gamblingcommission.gov.uk, Gambling Commission, Victoria Square House, Victoria Square, Birmingham B2 4BP, tel 0121 230 6720, email info@gamblingcommission.gov.uk.

The Health & Safety Executive and Health & Safety Commission publish guides to good practice and offer advice on how to comply with health and safety law. The HSE leaflet 'Five Steps to Risk Assessment' is highly recommended: www.hse.gov.uk.

Know the Score offers free and confidential information and advice about drugs: www.knowthescore.info, confidential information and advice helpline 0800 587 5879.

A Licensing Board is one of the main sources of information on the licensing law. It can provide the list of relevant and foreign offences that will be considered for licence applications, mandatory, discretionary and local conditions that apply to your premises, and acceptable forms of proof of age.

A local Licensing Forum is a statutory body set up to review the operation of licensing law and the local Licensing Board's function in the area. It represents a wide range of interests, including the licensed trade.

The Licensing (Scotland) Act 2005, Alcohol etc. (Scotland) Act 2010, Criminal Justice and Licensing (Scotland) Act 2010 and various accompanying regulations and updates are available to view or print out at www.legislation.gov.uk. You can order a copy from The Stationery Office Limited, PO Box 29, Norwich NR3 1GN, tel 0870 600 5522, email book.orders@tso.co.uk, www.tso.co.uk/bookshop.

A Licensing Standards Officer (LSO) is an excellent source of information and advice on the licensing legislation and how to ensure that your premises meets all of its responsibilities. The LSO can give advice on the kind of staff

training that you should be offering and the records that you should keep, as well as acceptable forms of proof of age and many other areas. The LSO is normally located in a department of your local council.

PPL, formally known as Phonographic Performance Limited, licences recorded music which is played in public or broadcast and distributes the licence fees to the performer and recording rightholder members: www.ppluk.com, tel 020 7534 1000, email info@ppluk.com.

PRS for Music (formerly Performing Rights Society) is the United Kingdom association of composers, songwriters and music publishers. It is a good source of information on music copyright: www.prsformusic.com, PRS for Music, 2 Pancras Square, London N1C 4AG, tel 020 7580 5544, fax 020 7306 4455.

Police, local, can help in many ways. Your police Community Involvement Department can arrange a drugs talk or training session run by a qualified expert. Your local police can also help you identify your premises drugs risk, and can advise on appropriate security measures. The Crime Prevention Officer can give advice on what you can do to deter theft, low-level crime and vandalism. The police can also put you in touch with Community Safety Partnerships, City Centre Safe groups, and your local Pubwatch or Retail Link.

Pubwatch is a community-based crime prevention scheme organised by the licensees themselves. National Pubwatch is a voluntary organisation set up to support existing pubwatches and encourage the creation of new pubwatch schemes, with the aim of achieving a safer social drinking environment: www.nationalpubwatch.org.uk, National Pubwatch PO Box 3523, Barnet, EN5 9LQ, tel 020 8775 3222, email admin@nationalpubwatch.org.uk.

The Red Cross (British) offers basic and advanced first aid training at centres throughout the UK: www.redcrossfirstaidtraining.co.uk, British Red Cross Society, Bradbury House, 4 Ohio Avenue, Salford Quays M50 2GT, tel 0844 871 8000, fax 0844 412 2739.

Retail Link is a network of voluntary local groups organised to reduce retail crime by sharing information among themselves and with the local police.

The Royal Environmental Health Institute of Scotland promotes the advancement of health, hygiene and safety in Scotland and is a good source of information on food hygiene: www.rehis.com, The Royal Environmental Health Institute of Scotland, 19 Torphichen Street, Edinburgh EH3 8HX, tel 0131 229 2968, fax 0131 228 2926, email contact@rehis.com.

The Scottish Drugs Forum is a national non-government drugs policy and information agency. It publishes booklets and leaflets such as *Know the Score*, *Where to Get Help: Directory of Services*, and *Drugs: What Every Parent Should Know*, and can help you, for instance, to assess your drugs risk: www.sdf.org.uk, Scottish Drugs Forum, 91 Mitchell Street, Glasgow G1 3LN, tel 0141 221 1175, fax 0141 248 6414, email enquiries@sdf.org.uk.

The Scottish Schools and Adolescent Lifestyle and Substance Use Survey (SALSUS) was established by the Scottish Executive to provide a broad approach to the monitoring of substance use in the context of other lifestyle, health and social factors: www.isdscotland.org/Health-Topics/Public-Health/SALSUS, Information Services Division, NHS National Services Scotland, Gyle Square, 1 South Gyle Crescent, Edinburgh EH12 9EB , tel 0131 275 7777.

The Security Industry Authority (SIA) manages the licensing of the private security industry as set out in the Private Security Industry Act 2001. It also aims to raise standards of professionalism and skills within the private security industry: www.sia.homeoffice.gov.uk, Security Industry Authority, PO Box 1293, Liverpool L69 1AX, tel 0844 892 1025, fax 0844 892 0975.

Smoke Free Scotland provides information and guidance on smoking legislation: www.clearingtheairscotland.com, smokeline Scotland 0800 848484.

The St Andrew's Ambulance Association offers first aid training ranging from two hours' tuition on basic resuscitation skills to week-long courses for first aiders in the workplace: www.firstaid.org.uk, St Andrew's First Aid, St Andrew's House, 48 Milton Street, Glasgow G4 0HR, tel 0141 332 4031, fax 0141 332 6582.

A Trading Standards Officer, local, can provide more information about requirements under the Weights and Measures and Trades Description Acts.

Books

Workbook for Staff of Licensed Premises, Alcohol Focus Scotland and City & Guilds: an excellent resource to use to record staff training. To obtain copies, email centresupport@cityandguilds.com, phone 0844 543 0000 or visit www.cityandguildsbookshop.com. Workbook can also be bought from Amazon.

Relevant courses

Certificate in Providing Security Services (Door supervision) (2915-02), City & Guilds

Conflict Management (2884), City & Guilds

First Aid, offered by both the British Red Cross and St Andrew's Ambulance Association (contact details above)

ServeWise Licensing Board Members' Qualification, Alcohol Focus Scotland

ServeWise Licensing Standards Officers' Qualification, Alcohol Focus Scotland

Scottish Certificate for Personal Licence Holders (7104-11), City & Guilds

Scottish Certificate for Personal Licence Holders (Refresher) at SCQF Level 6 (7104-21), City & Guilds

Hospitality and Catering: City & Guilds offer a range of qualifications, from entry level to advanced, on all aspects of hospitality and catering

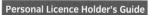

Test practice answers

1 Licensing law

1 c   The Licensing Board

2 a   A premises licence holder, a personal licence holder or a representative of a voluntary organisation

3 a   The premises is not meeting one of the licensing objectives

4 b   The Licensing Board

5 c   Every five years

6 b   At each place where sales of alcohol are made and at all times

7 b   The police must give notice to a person responsible for the premises

2 Other key legislation

1 a   It must be reviewed at regular intervals

2 c   To ensure that their working practices maintain the health and safety of themselves and their colleagues

3 b   To sell food that is past its 'best before' date

4 a   Advertisements should be socially responsible

3 Alcohol

1 a   1 (Increased risk of becoming a victim of crime), 3 (Death from alcohol poisoning), 4 (Short-term memory loss)

2 b   20 minutes

3 c   People are more vulnerable to accidents

4 c   Water and flavourings

4 Managing the premises and people

1 b   Other customers becoming involved

2 d   Phone the police on 999

3 b   1 (Acknowledge customers when they enter the premises), 3 (Operate a 'no proof, no sale' policy)

4 a   Be friendly to customers and make it clear what standards you expect of them

Acknowledgements

City & Guilds would like to sincerely thank Linda Bowie and Gillian Bell at Alcohol Focus Scotland for their expertise.

Picture credits

Every effort has been made to acknowledge all copyright holders as below and the publishers will, if notified, correct any errors in future editions.

Alcohol Focus Scotland: pp29, 92, 102; **Jane Smith**: pp58, 74; **Shutterstock**: © Africa Studio p46; © Ammentorp Photography p84; © B. and E. Dudzinscy p44; © Blend Images p84; © CandyBox Images pp16, 62, 81; © Chase Clausen p17; © Christian Bertrand p41; © Christian Delbert p12; © Claudio Divizia p92; © d13 p9; © Denphumi p60; © Digital Genetics p65; © dotshock p61; © Elena Elisseeva p48; © Elena Yakusheva p103; © Evgeny Karandaev pp45, 70; © Fanfo p17; © Fred Sweet p71; © Golden Pixels LLC pp81, 86; © Inga Ivanova p57; © Krystyna Kaczmarek p47; © Kzenon p89; © Lasse Kristensen p102; © Lorenz Timm p29; © luckyraccoon p12; © Marcio Jose Bastos Silva p85; © Martin Muránsky p51; © Meng Luen p28; © Minerva Studio p12; © Monkey Business Images p44; © Olaf Speier p71; © Peter Gudella p41; © Pindyurin Vasily p51; © Pressmaster p58; © sander p13; © senk p86; © sergign p86; © Stocklite p9; © StudioFI p93; © Valerie Potapova p51.

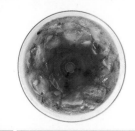

Notes